🍂 History *of* Britain 🍂

Food and Farming

Andrew Langley

Illustrated by M. Bergin, J. Field, J. James, B. Donohoe

Heinemann

HISTORY OF BRITAIN – FOOD AND FARMING
was produced for Heinemann Children's Reference
by Lionheart Books, London.

Editor: Lionel Bender
Designer: Ben White
Editorial Assistant: Madeleine Samuel
Picture Researcher: Jennie Karrach
Media Conversion and Typesetting: MW Graphics
Educational Consultant: Jane Shuter
Editorial Advisors: Andrew Farrow, Paul Shuter

Production Controller: David Lawrence

First published in Great Britain in 1997 by
Heinemann Educational Publishers, a division of Reed
Educational and Professional Publishing Limited,
Halley Court, Jordan Hill, Oxford OX2 8EJ.

MADRID ATHENS
FLORENCE PRAGUE WARSAW
PORTSMOUTH NH CHICAGO SAO PAULO MEXICO
SINGAPORE TOKYO MELBOURNE AUCKLAND
IBADAN GABORONE JOHANNESBURG KAMPALA NAIROBI

ISBN 0431 05723 0 Hb   ISBN 0431 05732 X Pb

British Library Cataloguing-in-Publication Data.
A catalogue record for this book is available
from the British Library.

Printed in Hong Kong by Wing King Tong Company Limited

Most of the artwork in this book has been published in other titles in the
History of Britain series.

Acknowledgements
Picture credits
Pages: 4: Michael Holford. 5: C. M. Dixon. 6: Lesley and Roy Adkins
Picture Library. 8-9: The Bridgeman Art Library/British Library, London
Add 42130 f.208. 9: Martyn F. Chillmaid. 10: The Bridgeman Art
Library/British Library, London. Add 42130 f.207. 11: Fotomas Index.
12: The Bridgeman Art Library/British Library, London. Add 18855
f.109. 13, 14: Fotomas Index. 15-16: © Crown Copyright, Historic Royal
Palaces. 16: Fotomas Index. 17: Michael Holford. 18: The National Trust
Photographic Library/Angelo Hornak. 19: Fotomas Index. 20-21: Fine Art
Photographic Library Ltd. 21: Mary Evans Picture Library/Illustrated
London News. 22: The National Trust Photographic Library/Will Curwen.
23: Mary Evans Picture Library/Illustrated London News. 24: Mary Evans
Picture Library. 25: Fine Art Photographic Library Ltd. 26: Hulton Deutsch
Collection Limited. 27: Robert Opie Collection. 28: Mary Evans Picture
Library. 28-29: Safeway Ltd plc.

Artwork credits
Main illustrators: Mark Bergin, John James, James Field.
Additional illustrations by Bill Donohoe.

Cover: Artwork by Mark Bergin, Bill Donohoe, John James and
Gerald Wood.

INTRODUCTION

There are three ways of getting enough to eat – hunting, growing or buying food. The first people to live in Britain were hunters. They gathered wild plants or killed game. Then came the first farmers, who grew their food. They planted crops and kept sheep and cattle. Later invaders introduced new and better ways of farming. Increasingly, people bought their food from others. In the 1600s, travellers to the New World of America brought back new kinds of food. But since Victorian times the population of Britain has been so big that farmers cannot grow enough to feed everyone. Today, Britain imports much of the food it needs.

CONTENTS

HUNTERS AND FARMERS

About 400,000 years ago, the first people came to Britain from Europe. They ate whatever food they could find. Some hunted deer and wild pigs. Some ate plant shoots and fruits. Others gathered shellfish from the seashore.

By about 6,000 BC, early Britons had made two great discoveries. One was that food tasted better when it was cooked over a fire. The second was a simple kind of farming. People began to clear patches in the woodland that covered much of Britain. They found that juicy young plants grew in these clearings. Deer and wild cattle came to feed there and were easier to catch.

The first proper farmers arrived in Britain in about 3,500 BC. They brought seeds for new plants, such as wheat and barley, which they sowed in clearings, and also sheep, pigs and goats.

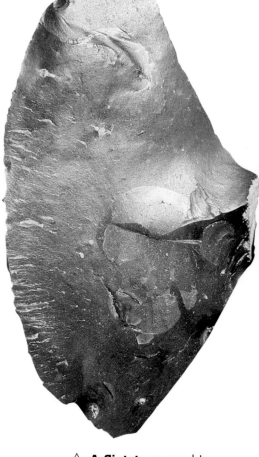

△ **A flintstone** used to scrape flesh from animals skins.

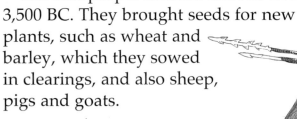

◁ **Hunters cut up a deer with knives made of flint**. They have killed their prey with spears or with arrows fired from bows. The arrows and spears have flint tips.

△ **Meat is cooked over a wood fire.** All the meat was eaten. The skin was used for clothing or shelters. The bones and horns were made into tools.

◁ **Early farmers** dig up ground for crops using wooden picks.

▷ **Wild pigs** and other animals were domesticated, or tamed, to keep on the farms.

Hunters had to wander in search of game, but farmers lived differently. They settled in one place and built houses. They cleared more land for crops, and put up fences to keep in their cattle. Men usually did the ploughing and looked after the animals. Women gathered wild food, such as nuts, and did the cooking. Everyone helped to harvest the crops.

◁ **A woman cooks** a stew of meat, water and herbs. The iron pot hangs over the fire from a hook. By the fire is a clay water pot.

◁ (Below) **A round hut on a farm** in about 500 BC. Farmers stored grain in pits nearby, to use in the winter.

▽ **The remains of a farm settlement** in Devon, from 650 BC.

VILLAS AND VINES

In AD 43 the Romans invaded Britain. They brought with them new farming tools and new kinds of food. During the next three centuries, the Romans built new towns and roads, too. And the invading army and the people in the new towns all had to be fed.

The Romans increased the area of farmland so that more crops could be grown. Even marshy areas were drained and ploughed up. Roman soldiers also raised their own farm animals at their forts, such as those along Hadrian's Wall.

△ **Fruit and vegetables** from local farms were sold in the towns. Shoppers could also buy fresh meat and bread. Some shops sold shellfish which were kept alive in tanks of water.

▷ **Copies of Roman pottery tableware** and glassware, and various Roman foods.

▽ **A donkey turns a mill wheel** to crush wheat into flour.

◁ **A Roman villa** was a farm, with a house and barns. Inside the villa walls were gardens with fruit trees and herbs. Outside were the fields for grain and vegetables.

▽ **The kitchen of a Roman villa** was well equipped to produce complicated meals.
• The charcoal and wood fire is raised on a hearth of brick or stone.
• The cooking pot stands on a metal grid.
• Liquids, such as the popular garum (a fish sauce), are kept in jars.
• Vegetables and joints of meat are hung from hooks in the ceiling.
• Fresh water is carried in wooden buckets.

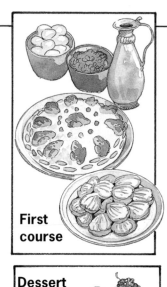

First course

Main course

Dessert

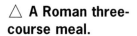

△ **A Roman three-course meal.**

◁ **At grand banquets,** guests ate lying on couches by the table. They used knives and spoons, or picked with their fingers. The meal might start with peacock eggs, stuffed olives and oysters. The main course might be boar's head, roast chicken and lobster. For dessert, there might be fruit, cakes and stuffed dates.

How do we know what people ate in Roman Britain? We can look at what they left behind. The bones of cattle, sheep and pigs have been found near army forts, showing that soldiers ate a lot of meat. They also loved shellfish. A pile of a million oyster shells was discovered at Silchester in Hampshire.

Wealthy Romans kept many unusual animals for food. Peacocks and pheasants, brought from Italy, were bred in pens. Dormice were put in special pots and fattened up with acorns and nuts. Snails were kept on tiny islands in ponds, so that they could not escape.

The Romans introduced many new kinds of vegetables and fruits to Britain. Among them were cabbages, onions, lettuce and turnips. The first orchards of apple and pear trees were planted by the Romans. But the invaders' favourite fruit was grapes. Grape pips have been found at many Roman sites, and there are several remains of vineyards in southern England. Most grapes were used to make wine, though huge loads of wine, in barrels or clay jars, were also carried by ship from France and Spain.

HARD WORK ON THE FARM

After the Romans left, Britain was split up among invaders from Ireland and Northern Europe. In England, Saxon kings shared out the best farmland among their most powerful warriors, or thanes, who in turn rented their land to peasant farmers, or churls.

Most churls rented a 'hide' of land – an area big enough to grow food for one family. Three or four of these family farms were grouped together. Some churls settled on farmland seized from the Britons. Others had to clear woodland and plough up new land for crops.

▷ **A Saxon monastery** of about AD 700. The monks had their own farm. There are fruit and vegetables in the gardens at the front. Cattle are kept in the sheds, and chickens in coops.

◁ **Saxon farmers** had to work hard all year round to grow enough food. Their main crops were wheat, oats and barley. They also grew peas, beans and lentils. In some years, the crops might fail because of drought. Cattle and sheep might die because of disease. Viking raiders might steal the food stores. Starvation was a constant threat.

8

◁ **A woman cooking in Jorvik** (York) in 870.

▷ **Viking settlers** often lived near the shore. They caught fish and preserved it by salting it or drying it in the open (far right).

Pigs, which then were thinner than modern breeds, were useful animals for Saxon farmers. They could live on rough land. The pigs were allowed to wander in the woods, where they ate nuts and roots. Goats were also happy there, eating leaves and brambles. But cattle and sheep needed young grass to eat. The farmers kept them on pasture land, which had been cleared of trees. Farmers had little winter food for cattle, so many of them were killed in the autumn.

Saxon farmers also used animals to help them. Oxen were yoked together in teams to pull the wheeled ploughs over the fields. Horses pulled the carts full of hay and other crops. Dogs guarded the sheep from wolves at night. Shepherds tied their dogs by ropes to their belts. If a dog saw a wolf, it would jerk at the rope and wake the shepherd.

▽ **A replica of foods in a Viking kitchen.** There are seabird eggs, dried meats and fish, bread and milk.

▽ **A 14th century illustration** showing a lord dining with his family at a long wooden table. A servant brings in dishes of food. On the table are bowls, plates, knives, spoons, bread and eggs. Forks were not yet used for eating.

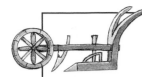

COMBATTING STARVATION

In medieval times, nine out of ten British people worked on the land. They had to. People were only able to grow the food they needed, and rarely had any to spare that they could sell or barter for other goods.

Most people were peasants, who lived in villages. All land in a village belonged to the lord of the manor. The peasants were bound to work for him, tilling his fields and harvesting his crops. In return, the lord gave them land for their own food.

▷ **Every village or manor** in Norman times had to grow all the food it needed. Only salt (used for preserving meat in winter) was bought from outside.

▷ **Stewing meat over a fire and chopping vegetables** – part of a medieval book illustration.

▽ **Domesday Book,** begun in 1086, was a survey of England. The king's officers visited villages, finding out who held each area of land and how it was used. Domesday Book showed that about two-thirds of the country was used for raising crops and animals.

Around the village were three or four large fields for growing crops. Each field was divided into long strips. The peasant families were allowed a certain number of strips in each field. In this way, good and bad land was shared out fairly. The peasants could only farm their own strips after they had finished work on the lord's land. This meant that they were very busy. Most peasants worked from dawn to dusk every day except for Sunday and holy days.

▷ **Peasants kept their animals fenced-off** in their houses. They stored hay and straw to feed the animals in winter. In summer, farm animals grazed on common land.

▽ **A boy scares birds** to stop them eating the seed in the newly-sown fields.

▷ **Wool became a valuable product** in medieval times. The fleeces were cut from sheep in early summer.

▽ **A woman spins thread** from wool while her husband breaks up the soil for sowing seeds.

△ **People ate food from wooden bowls** or sometimes from just thick pieces of bread, and drank ale or cider from leather mugs. They used knives to cut up bread and meat, and spoons made from cow's horns for pottage.

△ **Peasant food was simple.** Pottage, a thick broth with vegetables or meat, was served at most meals. So was bread, made from dark, coarse flour. The Church ordered that no-one should eat meat on three days each week.

Most cottages had only one room, and all cooking was done over a fire on a flat stone in the centre. Peasants baked their bread on small stones in the fire. Meat was usually boiled in an iron pot, but small animals, such as pigeons or even squirrels, were covered with clay and cooked in the hot ashes.

THE GARDEN GROWS

The most important animal in Tudor Britain was the sheep. By 1500, there were over 8 million sheep on the land – far more than people! Sheep were not kept for their meat, but for their wool, which was valuable.

△ **Wine in barrels.**

Rich farmers wanted more land for their sheep flocks. So they began to enclose the old open fields with hedges or fences. This meant that the villagers often had less land to grow crops or feed their animals. But in many areas farming life had hardly changed. Some farmers still dragged thorn bushes across ploughed fields to break up the soil. When its crop had been grown, a field was left fallow, or wild, for a whole year.

▽ **A village in late-Tudor times** (compare it with the picture on page 10). Can you see
• the windmill, where the wheat and barley were ground into flour;
• the fences round the enclosed fields in the distance;
• the shepherd tending his flock of sheep;
• the vegetable garden behind the church;
• the tithe barn below the church? (All villagers had to give a tithe, or tenth, of their produce to the Church. It was stored in the big tithe barn.)

▽ **Many different animals were killed for meat,** such as deer, rabbits and pigeons.

▽ **In winter,** many animals were killed and preserved in salt in wooden barrels.

▽ **Herbs and spices** were used in cooking to cover the rotten taste of old meat.

▷ **Sheep shearing on a Tudor farm** – from an illustrated manuscript of about 1540. Sheep were kept for meat as well as wool. As there were no freezers, food had to be preserved so that it would last a long time. Most meats were salted or 'smoked' by hanging them in a chimney. Eggs were covered with wax and buried in sawdust. Milk was made into cheese.

△ **Poor people** ate coarse bread (often made from acorns), with butter, eggs and bacon, and drank ale or cider.

△ **Rich people** ate bread made with white flour, and sweetened their food with sugar. They drank wine.

△ **Town-workers** mostly lived, slept, cooked and ate in the same room. Soup and meat was cooked over an open fire. Breakfast, of bread and soup or meat, was eaten early. Lunch was often bought in a tavern or from a nearby 'cookshop'. Supper, in the early evening, was usually bread and cheese with ale.

△ **A rich family eats together.** In poor families, the husband would eat only when the day's work was done.

By the end of the sixteenth century, there were many more vegetable and fruit gardens. Every country house had garden beds for beetroot, parsnips and onions. New fruits from Europe and Asia, such as quinces and apricots, were trained against walls.

Herbs were important to give flavour to dishes and as medicines. Gardeners laid out herb beds in knot patterns, decorated with flowers. Only the wealthy could afford spices, such as cloves, which came from the Far East.

13

ROYAL FEASTS

Tudor kings and queens ate splendid food – and spent thousands of pounds on it. When Henry VIII was with his court at Nonsuch Palace, there were 1,500 followers and servants to feed each day. Nobles also had to provide food for their large households.

All this cooking needed many people (Elizabeth I's kitchens had a staff of over 160). And it took up a lot of space. Each great Tudor house had its own kitchens (for cooking and preparing food), larders (for storing food), cellars (for keeping wine), dairy and bakehouse. At feasts, most of the diners sat in the great hall, the largest room in the house. But the lord, his family and important friends ate together in a private room.

◁ **Monasteries** had been centres of farming as well as religion for nearly 1,000 years. But in 1536, Henry VIII began to dissolve, or close down, the monasteries. He made a fortune selling church land and used much of it to pay for his grand houses and big feasts.

◁ (Inset) **Monks** eat a simple meal together in the monastery refectory.

△ **Henry VIII hunting with his hawk.** The hawk was released to catch rabbits and partridges. Hunting was a popular sport for noblemen (and women – Elizabeth I often rode after deer). The game, including herons, hares and even swans, was often served at feasts.

◁ **'The House of Rest'.** This Tudor illustration shows a merchant sitting down to a meal at an inn. The inn-keeper's wife cooks meat over the fire. Inns provided the monarch's followers with places to eat, drink and sleep along the way when they moved from one palace to another.

△ **Stuffed peacock,** one of the grand dishes enjoyed by Tudor monarchs.

▷ **Henry VIII dines in his chamber.** Servants bring in food and musicians play.

At a royal feast, guardsmen might carry in as many as twenty dishes for every course. Each guard was given a mouthful to eat, to make sure that none of the food was poisoned. After the main meal came the 'banquet' – a colourful course of sweets, such as animals made of sugar and marzipan. Special banqueting houses were built on roofs or in gardens.

◁ **The kitchens at Hampton Court,** built by King Henry VIII's chancellor Thomas Wolsey. In front is a wooden table on which food was prepared then placed on pewter plates and in clay jars like those on the tabletop. Behind the table is the fireplace where food was cooked.

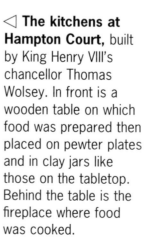

△ **Dishes are carried to a nobleman's great hall.** Wealthy people ate their food from gold or silver plates. Forks were now being used more often.

NEW WORLD, NEW FOOD

During Tudor and Stuart times, European explorers found new sea routes to America and the Far East. They brought back many kinds of food. From America came sweetcorn, pumpkins, potatoes and chocolate. From the Far East came tea and spices.

At first, British settlers in North America found farming hard, and many of them starved. They had to learn how to catch game and grow crops like the Indians.

▷ **An early British colony in North America.** Like the first settlers in Britain, these pioneers had to clear fields to sow crops.

▷ **A ship carrying settlers to America.**

▷ (Centre) **Turkeys and corn** were two New World foods which were brought to Europe.

▷ (Far right) **Tobacco from America** made smoking fashionable.

▽ **In the early 17th century,** King James I wrote a pamphlet against the practice of smoking tobacco.

▷ **Unloading food at a new settlement** in America. Until settlers could grow enough crops and tame animals, they had to bring food from Britain.

The seas around the east coast of North America contained huge numbers of fish, especially cod. Fishermen from Britain and other European countries crossed the Atlantic to catch them. The fish was salted and packed in barrels during the voyage home. Cod became a more important food in Britain – and still is today.

◁ **Sailors from Bristol** fishing with nets for the cod which swarmed in the shallow seas off the coast of Newfoundland (Canada).

▽ **Many new crops** were brought from South America, including coffee and potatoes. Potatoes, probably brought by Francis Drake, were soon grown in Scotland and Ireland, becoming the main food crop there. Tomatoes did not become popular until much later.

▷ **African slaves** were brought to the West Indies to work on sugar plantations.

▽ **Sugar cane from the West Indies** was shipped to Britain, where it was refined. The sugar was sold in big pieces. It was used in fruit dishes.

During the seventeenth century, British explorers and merchants began making longer voyages in search of new lands and trade. They needed to take a large supply of food which would last many weeks without spoiling. The most usual rations were salted beef, dried peas and bread. Some took smoked hams covered in honey or pine tar to keep out air and flies (and pork fat was used as a kind of sun cream!). Live hens provided eggs, and goats gave fresh milk.

A FARMING REVOLUTION

Between 1700 and 1850, the population of Britain soared from 9 million to 28 million. The reason for this was more food. Improved methods of farming allowed greater quantities and quality of food to be produced. As a result, food was cheaper to buy.

Farmers found new ways of making their land more fertile. They put marl (a kind of clay) on light soil to make it hold greater amounts of water. They grew clover and special grasses, which added goodness to the soil. And they hoed between the rows of crops to keep down weeds.

An important new crop was turnips. In winter, cattle and sheep were put on to turnip fields to feed. This, with better hay and grain, solved the problem of keeping animals through the winter. Now, far fewer had to be killed. Also, by careful breeding, farmers could rear better cattle, sheep and pigs.

△ **Jethro Tull built the first seed** drill in about 1701. This sowed seeds directly into the soil in rows. Before this, the seed had been scattered by hand, and a lot of it had been wasted.

▽ **A Hereford bull** – an improved breed of cattle. Fatter and healthier cattle like this were bred by pioneer farmers, such as Robert Bakewell of Leicestershire. He chose only the best animals in his herd to breed together. Sheep and pig breeds were also improved in this way to provide more meat.

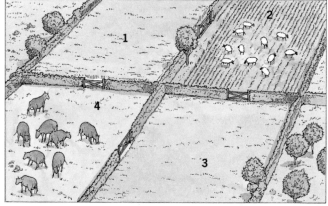

△ **The 'four-course' system of rotating crops.** For centuries, farmers had used only three courses. They had grown wheat one year, barley the next, and then left the field fallow, or empty, for a year to regain its fertility. The new system avoided this waste and used land all the time.

Year 1: Wheat, sowed in the autumn. **Year 2:** Turnips, used to feed cattle and sheep in winter. **Year 3:** Barley, sowed in the spring. **Year 4:** Grass and clover for cattle and sheep to graze on. The dung from the animals made the soil more fertile.

▽ **Farm workers plant a hedge** and enclose a field. People who lived on common land were forced to move out.

◁ **The Fens** (marshes) in Lincolnshire were drained, using windmills to pump away the water. The soil here was rich and ideal for growing grain and vegetables.

◁ **Turnips** were not the only winter feed. By 1800, many farmers were also giving cattle 'cake' made from crushed oil seeds.

The new farming changed the country-side, especially in England. Landowners had started to enclose, or fence off, the old open fields in Tudor times. Now enclosure speeded up. Between 1760 and 1815, over one million hectares of land were fenced with walls or hedges.

Villagers and small farmers had always used the common land for grazing their pigs, sheep and geese. Enclosure ruined their way of life and forced many to move to towns to find work. But it also made farming more efficient. Fences stopped animals from trampling on crops and spreading pests and diseases.

△ **Shepherds** use poles to push a flock of sheep into a stream in early summer. The men in the water are washing the fleeces of the sheep to clean them before they are shorn.

▷ **Laws allowing the enclosing of land,** and other new farming methods, threatened many people with losing their jobs. During the 1830s, protesters burned hayricks and smashed farm machines.

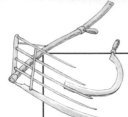

MACHINES ON THE FARM

"A curious, shapeless thing, with a man riding upon it, comes jerking forward, tearing its iron teeth deep through the earth." This was how Richard Jefferies described the sight of a steam plough in the 1870s. New machines like this revolutionized farming.

△ **Hand-power – a harvester** cuts down wheat with a sickle, which he keeps very sharp.

▽ (Bottom) **Wheat** is fed into the top of a steam powered thresher.

▽ **Machine-power – a steam plough** is pulled across the field by chains driven by a stationary steam engine.

The first all-steel plough had been built in 1837. It was still pulled by horses but was stronger than the old wooden plough. Its blade stayed sharp and did not get clogged with mud. Then iron rollers were introduced, to crush the lumps of soil, and chain harrows broke them up into smaller pieces.

During the 1850s, farmers began using horse-drawn reapers to cut down corn. Steam-powered threshers separated the grain from the straw. By the 1870s, the first steam tractors were at work.

△ **Horse-drawn carts** were still vital for moving all kinds of loads on the farm, such as cow and pig manure for the fields.

◁ **A horse pulling a cart** piled high with wheat from a harvest field. Children still worked as farm-hands.

Other inventions improved farmland, making it grow better crops. The 'mole plough' was dragged under the earth to make drainage channels in wet ground. Clay pipes made draining even simpler.

Scientists studied the way plants grew, and found that some chemicals present in animal bones and manure enriched the soil. Soon many farmers were using new fertilizers. Among these was seabird dung, called guano, which was imported from South America.

△ **A bustling market** in Lambeth, London, in 1872. The populations of towns were growing fast, and needed a huge amount of food.

◁ **Steam ploughs** only worked well on big, flat fields. On smaller farms, horses were used to pull ploughs until well into the twentieth century.

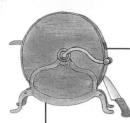

FRESH AND PRESERVED FOOD

By the 1850s, most British people could eat a bigger variety of food than ever before. Farms and gardens were growing more. Railways carried fresh food swiftly from the countryside to the towns. And new ways of milling and baking had made bread cheaper.

The revolution in farming soon spread into the gardens of homes. There, people could use fertilizers, lawn-mowers and hoses. Many new houses were built with space for a vegetable plot. But the most magnificent gardens of all served the big country houses. Sheltered by high walls, these gardens produced vegetables, fruit and flowers all the year round.

▽ **Goods are being loaded on to a train.** Railways could carry fresh milk and other farm produce to the towns every day.

△ **The high walls** round the huge kitchen garden at Wallington in Northumberland kept warmth in and winds out, helping plants grow more quickly. The glasshouses were heated in winter with hot water flowing through pipes.

▷ **A gardener** delivers a basket of fresh vegetables to a kitchen maid to prepare. All the house's fruit and vegetables were grown in the walled garden. In winter, apples, pears and other fruit were stored in a special shed. A garden like this needed a staff of 20 or more men and boys to keep it running. They grew an amazing variety of crops. Catalogues from the 1880s list 60 different kinds of peas, and over 500 different kinds of apple trees!

▷ **Food was usually cheaper to buy** in the towns than in country villages. City market stalls and shops competed with each other to gain customers, and kept their prices low.

▷ **Experiments with tinned food** were made in about 1817. Food was sealed in cans then heated to kill germs. In 1856, the Royal Navy set up its own canning factory to supply meat and vegetables for sailors.

◁ **Some cows were kept in the cities** and their milk was sold fresh each day.

△ **A shopkeeper** with a tin of biscuits. Many processed foods had colourful packages.

Meanwhile, people found new ways to preserve foods. The earliest freezers were 'ice houses', where food was packed in ice hacked from frozen ponds in winter. By 1880, meat was being sent to Britain from America in chilled containers. Mutton (sheep meat) sealed in cans came from Australia. Shoppers could also buy food that had not been grown on farms but made in factories. Custard powder, self-raising flour, margarine, dried soup and bottles of sauce were among the first of these 'processed' foods.

RICH, POOR OR MIDDLE-CLASS?

In 1864, a doctor wrote: "In very poor families, the children are fed at breakfast and supper chiefly with bread. At dinner they have the same food or boiled potato or cabbage." These people had no stove or running water for preparing and cooking food.

▽ **A menu** showing what people might have eaten at a grand formal dinner, such as the one drawn by Richard Doyle in 1864 (bottom). This picture, called *A State Party*, shows Queen Victoria (seen from behind), government ministers, rich guests, waiters and poor onlookers.

At the same time, richer people could afford much better food. At dinner parties, they showed off their wealth by serving expensive and complicated dishes. By the 1880s, this meal might consist of twelve courses, including soup, fish, meat and three different desserts.

In between the rich and poor were the middle classes. They were better off than ever before, and wanted to copy the eating habits of the wealthy. The middle classes did not grow their own food but bought it from shops or from the traders who sold vegetables and fish at the door.

△ **Afternoon tea** was a new kind of meal for wealthy or middle-class families. They drank tea and ate thin sandwiches, cakes and biscuits.

MENU

Potage à la Reine.

Saumon.

Côtelette de Veau.

Pommes de terre.
Petits Pois.
Charlotte Russe.

△ **Mealtimes** for middle-class Victorians were formal – and filling!
• Breakfasts might include pies, meat, eggs and muffins

• Lunch was lighter, with cold meats and salads
• Dinner started at 8 pm. Meat was put on a dish in the kitchen then brought to the table to be carved.

▷ **Working-class** Victorians had simple meals. Dinner might be cold meat slices, bread and butter, and tea.

▽ **Most Victorians were religious** and usually said 'Grace' before meals, as this painting shows.

At the beginning of the Victorian Age, many kitchens had a cast-iron 'range' for cooking. This had an open coal fire with an oven next to it. By the 1850s, many people were using the new closed range, which had a hot-plate over the fire. Gas began to replace coal for heating.

Gadgets made the cook's life much easier. Food could be kept fresh in early refrigerators, which were special large cupboards packed with ice. Other useful Victorian inventions were mincers, coffee grinders, knife sharpeners, food mixers and bread slicers. The very first tea-making machine, attached to an alarm clock, was built in 1891.

WAR AND RATIONING

By 1914, the population of the British Isles had risen to over 43 million. Farmers could not grow enough to feed this many people, so a lot of food had to be bought from abroad by ship. For example, three-quarters of the wheat for bread was imported.

△ **Ration books** were issued to everyone at the start of the Second World War. The coupons inside were cut out when an item was purchased.

▽ **Plenty of fresh food** is being grown in this 1940s suburban garden. There are chickens, as well as vegetables, herbs and fruit trees.

During the First World War (1914 – 1918), the German Navy attacked and sank many ships carrying food to Britain. Several kinds of food began to run short. By 1917, there was only enough food to last the country for three weeks. The government limited the amount of meat, flour and other foods that people could buy. This was called rationing.

When the Second World War broke out in 1939, rationing began right away. Among the first foods to be rationed were butter, meat and fresh eggs.

▽ **Growing vegetables** on an allotment set up in 1942 on the site of a house destroyed by a German bomb. Crops were grown on every available piece of land.

▽ **An adult's weekly ration of food** (below right) included 4 ounces (112 grams) of butter, 14 old pence-worth (about £2 today) of meat, and 12 ounces (336 grams) of sugar.

▽ **Queuing to buy food.** The government urged people to buy preserved food, such as dried eggs.

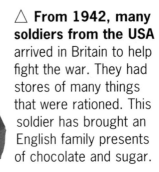

△ **From 1942, many soldiers from the USA** arrived in Britain to help fight the war. They had stores of many things that were rationed. This soldier has brought an English family presents of chocolate and sugar.

During 1942, the Germans sank 8 million tonnes of shipping. Food was again running dangerously short. Besides rationing, the British government encouraged people to 'Dig For Victory'. Extra land, including parks and playing fields, was ploughed up to grow crops. People grew vegetables instead of flowers in their gardens.

▷ **Hundreds of city shops were damaged** or destroyed by German bombs during raids known as the Blitz. But people were determined to keep going. Shop-keepers patched up broken windows and walls and put up signs saying 'Business as Usual'.

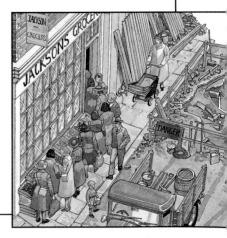

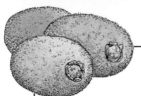

FACTORY FARMS, FAST FOOD

The Second World War was good for British farmers. People saw how important it was to grow as much food as possible at home. Since the war, farmers have been helped by government money to become more efficient, with new machines, methods and chemicals.

Today, everything is done on a big scale. Huge tractors haul wide ploughs and cultivators. Tonnes of fertilizer (made in factories) are spread over the land. Drills sow twelve or more lines of seeds at the same time. Chemical sprays kill off the weeds.

Vast combine harvesters are used to cut down the crop, separate the grains and throw out the straw at the back. To make room for such monster machines, hedges and walls have been ripped out.

▽ **This chemical sprayer** stretches for 6 metres on each side of the tractor. Grain from these vast fields is stored in the tall silo in the background.

△ **An advertisement for an electric refrigerator**, from 1951. At this time, only a few Britons could afford a 'fridge'. Today, most homes have one. Modern homes have other kitchen gadgets, too. Freezers, microwave ovens, toasters, electric kettles and food mixers have all helped to make cooking easier, quicker and cleaner than ever before.

▷ **Cans of food on a factory line.** Factories like this can process huge amounts of food without stopping. The food is cleaned, prepared and partly cooked. Then it is put into the cans, sealed and heated to a high temperature to complete the cooking and destroy germs.

◁ **Shoppers can buy an amazing range of foods** from all over the world in a modern supermarket. Among these are:
• Coffee from Central America
• Meat from New Zealand
• Rice from the USA
• Tomatoes from Italy
• Tea from India
• Apples from Australia
• Cheese from France
• Chocolate from Switzerland
• Fruit from South Africa.

In spite of this farming revolution, a lot of Britain's food comes from overseas. There are many ways of preserving meat, fish, vegetables and fruit so that they can be sent cheaply over long distances without 'going off', or rotting, on the way. Frozen, canned or dried food will last for many months. Most preserved food contains extra chemicals that prevent harmful germs from developing. Some people think that these chemicals are themselves a danger to health.

Much fresh food also comes from abroad. Aircraft carry vegetables and fruit in chilled compartments across the world in a few hours. This kind of food goes rotten very quickly, so some of it is treated with special light to stop decay. In spite of this costly treatment, imported food can be cheaper than home-grown produce. In 1997, strawberries from California cost less than English ones!

△ **Most eggs in Britain** are laid by hens kept in cages with wire floors and no natural light. Their eggs roll on to a conveyor belt that takes them away to be packed. Other farm animals, such as pigs, sometimes spend their whole lives in heated concrete sheds.

△ **Many people believe that this 'factory farming'** is cruel and that the drugs given to some farm animals to 'fatten them up' harm those people who eat their meat. For safety, some farmers now allow hens to roam 'free range' over a field.

△ **The most popular 'meal'** in Britain is 'fast food' – such as the American beef burger. Burgers from shops are quick to buy and easy to eat. Along with chips and sugary drinks, this kind of food is fattening and may encourage heart disease.

PLACES TO VISIT

Here are some sites relating to food and farming in Britain. Your local Tourist Office will be able to tell you about other places in your area.

Acton Scott Historic Working Farm, Shropshire. Shows the way people farmed in Victorian times.
Baxters of Speyside, Grampian. Find out how soup and haggis are made on a guided tour of a food factory.
Butser Farm, Hampshire. A reconstructed Iron Age farm.
Chedworth Villa, Gloucestershire. Remains of a Roman villa showing the kitchen area.
Chesters Fort, Hexham. A well-preserved Roman cavalry fort with eating and kitchen area.
Erddig, Clwyd. Eighteenth-century house with perfectly preserved kitchens.
Felin Crewi Watermill, Powys. A working water-powered flour mill.
Haddon Hall, Derbyshire. Includes a grand medieval banqueting hall.
Hampton Court Palace, Surrey. Has magnificent Tudor kitchens.
Jorvik Viking Centre, York. Excavated city shows how the Vikings cooked and ate, among many other things.
Longleat House, Wiltshire. Contains a perfect Victorian kitchen.

Museum of London, London. Many exhibits show Londoners' eating habits through history.
North of England Open Air Museum, Tyne and Wear. A recreated town from around 1913.
Skara Brae, Orkney. Stone Age village which shows how people lived and ate.
Ulster History Park, Co. Tyrone. Reconstructions of Ulster life from 8000 BC.
West Stow, Suffolk. Reconstruction of an Anglo-Saxon village.

FURTHER READING

Here are some books that will tell you more about the history of food and farming in Britain. You will find these, and others, in your local or school library.

The British Kitchen by Doreen Yarwood, Batsford, 1981.
The Field Guide: A Farmland Companion by John Woodward and Peter Luff, Blandford, 1983.
Food in England by Dorothy Hartley, Macdonald, first published in 1954.
A Taste of History: 10,000 Years of Food in Britain by Peter Brears and others, English Heritage/British Museum, 1993.

GLOSSARY

bakehouse A room or building where bread is baked in ovens.

banquet Usually a grand meal, with lots of food.

barley A grain crop used for food and for making beer and whisky.

Britons People who were living in Britain before the Roman and Saxon invasions.

class The group in society that a person belongs to. In the past, these were (in order from the highest, or richest): nobles, gentry, craftsmen, yeomen, peasants, the poor. Today, the order is: upper class, middle class and lower, or working, class.

colony Land in one country that is ruled by another country.

common land Land which is not owned by anyone, and which can be used by everyone.

cookshop A shop where cooked food can be bought.

cultivator A farming tool used instead of a plough, which breaks up the soil without turning it.

dairy The place on a farm where milk is stored. Here the cream is taken off the milk and made into cheese.

dessert The last course in a lunch or dinner, usually a sweet.

enclosure The fencing in of open common land with hedges and walls.

famine A disastrous shortage of food.

fertilizer A substance put on the soil which gives plants the right foods and chemicals to help them grow.

fleece The wool of a sheep.

flint A hard mineral that can be split to make a sharp edge.

game Wild animals hunted for food or sport.

glasshouse A building covered with glass for growing plants in; it lets in light but keeps the plants warm.

import To bring in goods, such as food, from another country.

lord A noble or king, a person who was owed loyalty by his followers.

merchant A person who makes their living by buying and selling things, either in their own country or abroad.

monarch The ruler of a country – the king or queen.

monastery A place where monks live together after taking religious vows.

peasant A farmer or labourer who works on the land.

plantation A large farm growing one crop, such as sugarcane or bananas.

range A cooking stove with surfaces and ovens on which you can cook several things at once.

rationing The sharing out of goods, especially food, which are in short supply so that everyone gets an equal share.

sickle A tool with a short, curved blade using for cutting grain or tall grass.

slave A person held captive and forced to work for no pay.

taxes Money collected by a lord or the government from the people, to pay for new roads, buildings or to equip an army.

tilling Preparing the soil for growing crops.

villa A large country house with a farm.

vineyard A field where grapevines are grown.

wheat A grain used for making bread, cakes and pasta.

working class People who were seen as poor and unimportant in Victorian times. These people had to work for others to earn a living – they were employees. Miners, shopworkers, servants, factory workers were working class.

INDEX

to instruct and inspire

To Instruct and Inspire accompanies an exhibition of art and crafts which coincides with the launch of the 125th anniversary celebrations of The University of Wales, Aberystwyth in October 1997. This illustrated guide examines the nature of the University's collection, its development and the individuals whose personal enthusiasms have shaped the art and crafts collection over the past 125 years. The University has never been able to fund its own art and crafts museum, nor today does it benefit from 'special factor' government funding enjoyed by some of the larger university museums in England. All our achievements have only been made possible through the generosity of our benefactors: George Powell of Nanteos, Gwendoline and Margaret Davies of Llandinam, Sir John Williams, Dr Elvet Lewis, and the friends and former students of the University too numerous to name here, who have contributed financially or made individual gifts and bequests of works of art.

Today, probably more than ever before, the art and crafts collections are making an invaluable contribution to the teaching and research activities of the School of Art and the curators who continue to generate publications and national touring exhibitions. In fact, it was not until the late 1970s and the first published research on the early history of the collections by Moira Vincentelli, that the University began to appreciate the extent, and indeed the significance, of the material in its possession. While many other departmental collections are no longer of relevance to teaching this is not the case with art and art history which are necessarily bound up with these specialised forms of material culture. Unlike the larger university museums, the Aberystwyth collections remain at the heart of teaching at the School of Art, primarily as a teaching and research resource for staff and students but with ever increasing public access. Since 1976 the policy has been to strengthen and develop the holdings of graphic art and studio ceramics. The collections of ceramics, prints and photographs in particular are not only unique in Wales but they are of international importance, and recently many items of great significance have been loaned to prestigious exhibitions throughout the UK, the Continent, America and Japan. These works are our ambassadors, they carry the name of The University of Wales, Aberystwyth across the world.

This exhibition to mark 125 years of collecting is particularly dedicated to those staff of the art department, past and present, who have voluntarily devoted much of their valuable time to the collections, and whose dedication and enthusiasm has been unstinting during times of continuing financial instability and hardship. We are indebted to Professors Rudler and Fleure, Sidney Greenslade and Dan Jones, Lambert Gapper and in recent years Alistair Crawford and Moira Vincentelli, without their selfless and often thankless endeavours on behalf of the University collections this exhibition could certainly never have taken place. As this century draws to a close we sincerely hope that new patrons will come forward to help us fulfil our vision for the new millennium, to build upon our recent successes in attracting significant teaching and research collections to Aberystwyth, and to take the collections into the international arena. George Powell, John Williams, the Davies sisters and Dr Thomas Jones, and Elvet Lewis all shared our loyalty towards the University and our commitment to the teaching, study and display of art in Wales. They also valued a fundamental need to broaden the students' cultural experience with, in the words of our forebears, 'a knowledge as well as a proper sense of appreciation of these "things of beauty", so that they may be able to instruct and inspire for the welfare of the coming generations'. (The Curators, *Annual Reports* 1925).

Robert Meyrick Senior Lecturer and Curator of Graphic Art & Neil Holland Assistant Curator
The University of Wales, Aberystwyth, School of Art, October 1997

Giovanni Piranesi (1920-78) *Antichita Romane* etching 1756

F W Rudler's box collection

Antonio Tempesta (1555-1630) *The Lion Hunt* etching c.1600

Anonymous *Ignatius of Loyola* oil [formerly in the Church of San Juan de Dios, Lima, Peru] Given by Charles Thomas,

The General Museum

the General Museum

One of the first museums in Britain to open its doors to the public was a university museum - the Ashmolean Museum, Oxford in 1683. Many of the larger universities have followed suit in the proceeding centuries and many more have small departmental teaching collections run by staff on a voluntary basis with limited public access. The collections at Aberystwyth have until recently always fallen into the latter category. There has been a museum of sorts since the foundation of the University College in 1872. The development of the Museum was principally the work of Frederick William Rudler (1840-1915), the Professor of Chemistry who became the Museum's first Curator in 1876. He was assisted by Professors Walter Keeping and J Mortimer Angus who collected, arranged and catalogued the mineralogical and geological material. Rudler was formerly assistant curator at the Museum of Practical Geology in London and apart from Chemistry, Physics, Geology, Botany and Zoology his interests encompassed the history of pottery making in Britain and Japanese art and crafts.

Rudler's intention was to found a central or national museum for Wales in Aberystwyth concentrating particularly on the mining industries and the processing of copper, lead, iron, silver and tin. In only three years he amassed large numbers of specimens by appeals for gifts. The displays of the new collections, in his own words, treated the subject 'popularly as well as educationally'. Rudler also amassed a great deal of geological, botanical and palaeontological material, some through an exchange of materials with other museums. The first substantial collection of ethnological material was given by Bryce Wright of London in the form of spears, clubs and paddles from Africa and Polynesia. In 1879, at the end of Rudler's short time as Curator, George E J Powell began to donate his collections, initially in the form of Roman and Egyptian antiquities and Japanes 'curios' .

Rudler left in 1879 to become Curator at the Museum of Practical Geology in London where he remained until his retirement in 1902. However he maintained his links with Aberystwyth; his personal collection was offered to the University and purchased in 1915 - including 3,000 pamphlets and publications on Geology, along with items of Romano-British and medieval pottery and glass. It also included a collection of tiny boxes in an assortment of materials - raffia-work, celluloid plastic, various woods, metals and lacquer - probably intended to illustrate a variety of substances and processes of manufacture, but which also indicate that he was an obsessive collector. Rudler's views on collecting and the role of the Museum are expressed in his article for the *College Magazine* (Vol.IV, 1882). In it he stresses the need to cater for public as well as scholarly interest in the presentation of exhibits. He also outlines the underlying scientific scheme in his own apparently heterogeneous collections: 'The old coin, the autograph or the pot-sherd may teach more of real vivid history than an ordinary student can learn from many pages of a book'. Such a statement anticipates a tenet dear to many latter-day students of material culture, not least art historians.

After 1879 the Museum was curated by the young Professor of Chemistry, Thomas Samuel Humpidge (c.1852-1887) who wrote *A Short Handbook to the Museum* (J E Cornish, Manchester 1881). Unfortunately it was from Humpidge's chemistry laboratories in the Old College that the fire of 1885 started, in which three men died in the Museum rooms. The majority of the Museum collection was saved but most of the records were lost. Professor Humpidge died at the age of 35, reportedly through the effects of overwork. At the time Professor J H Salter took over as Curator, soon after 1900, the entries for the Museum in the *Annual Reports* become brief and intermittent. Money raised from public admission charges to the Museum was used to create a 'Visitors' Scholarship' rather than invested in museum provision.

His successor Professor Hubert John Fleure (1877-1969) kept the Museum going in one form or another from c.1910 until 1929. Fleure, who was the first Professor of Geography in Britain, extracted enough voluntary support and money from the University for the continued existence of the Museum. His interests were as wide-ranging as Rudler's; he wrote many works on anthropology, most notably the *Corridors of Time* series written with Harold Peake (1867-1946). A humanist and a keen advocate of the ideas of William Morris, Fleure was eager for the Museum to promote the Arts & Crafts Movement's philosophy as part of a more broadly based educational provision for students, schoolchildren and local people.

It was to be an uphill struggle. In the *Annual Reports* (1913-14) he called for 'a full-time curator to develop it still further as a broadly cultural and artistic influence'. Fleure attracted significant gifts from the British Museum through F N Pryce in 1912, an ex-student working in the Department of Greek and Roman Antiquities, and from the famous archaeologist Margaret Murray who donated items from the digs she attended with Flinders Petrie. In 1917, however, the *Annual Reports* reveal Fleure's state of desperation, 'During the past session efforts have been made to maintain the organisation of the Museum in spite of a complete absence of help'. Fleure's often repeated hope that the Museum should be instrumental in 'liberalising' the students' education was in great danger of remaining unrealised until Gwendoline and Margaret Davies intervened with their generous gift to the Museum in the following year. **NH**

William Goscombe John (1860-1952)
Bokani plaster 1905

George Powell of Nanteos

George Powell photograph c.1860

In my will, therefore, I had left to your University - as well as being quite the worthiest and most intelligent corporate body in my dear but benighted town - all I possessed 'of bigotry and virtue'. (Letter GP to Principal T C Edwards, 4.iv.1879)

George Ernest John Powell (1842-1882) was the son of Colonel William Thomas Rowland Powell of Cheltenham (1815-1878), Member of Parliament for Cardiganshire (1859-1865), and Rosa Edwyna Powell (née Cherry) of Buckland, Herefordshire. His early years were spent at the family mansion of Nanteos three miles south of Aberystwyth. The family wealth was accrued from the profits of various lead and silver ore mines in Cardiganshire. George Powell was initially educated at home by his mother but sent to public school at Eton in the 1850s and in 1861 he matriculated to Brasenose College, Oxford but left before graduating. He spent most of his adult life in London and France and had sufficient means to pursue a life of travelling - throughout Europe, northern Africa and Iceland - writing poetry and indulging his passion for both music and collecting books, music manuscripts, autograph letters, fine and decorative art, coins and 'curiosities'. Powell succeeded to the Nanteos Estate in 1878, was made High Sheriff of Cardigan 1880-81, married Dinah T Harris a housekeeper of Goodwick, Pembrokeshire in 1881 and died on 17 October 1882.

Powell began giving his collections to the University in 1879 and bequeathed the rest on his death in 1882. In three letters to Principal Thomas Charles Edwards (4.iii.1879, 26.iv.1879, and 8.iv.1882) Powell sets out his intentions and lists some of the artefacts he wishes to donate - a 'tiny batch of Icelandic curios', a 'curious and unique' series of Japanese paintings on paper, 'some superb works' in jewelled and enamelled silver and some Japanese ivory carvings. He had approached the University as early as 1874, but now convinced of the stability of both the University and the Museum and apparently familiar with the curators he seems to have been spurred on to acquire artefacts specifically for the Museum.

Powell had offered his collection to the town initially in 1871 through the agency of the Rev. E O Phillips of Llanbadarn, with the proviso that a room or gallery was built to house it. At the time the collection was valued at £5,000. After a year of meandering discussion by the town council and an unsuccessful attempt to finance both a free public library and a gallery by implementation of the 1845 Public Libraries Act, Powell withdrew his offer - but not before the value and quality of the gift had been called into question. His collection was given to the University in the belief that its intrinsic value and usefulness in academic pursuits would be recognised in the eyes of both scholars and townspeople and that this would win him status in his life-time and a particular category of immortality.

Richard Westall (1765-1836) *The Birth of Sin* illustrating Milton's *Paradise Lost* watercolour 1790s

Clause 31 of Powell's will (16.X.1882) sets out the bequest: 'I give and bequeath to the trustees for the time being of the Museum of the said University College all my oil and watercolour paintings and crayon drawings not at Nanteos aforesaid and (hereinafter specially mentioned) whether the same paintings and drawings happen to be at 41 Mornington Crescent aforesaid at the time of my death or elsewhere under the care of Mr Smith Picture Dealer 137 New Bond Street or any other person. And I give and bequeath ... all the Roman Greek Egyptian and other antiquities and all curiosities and objects of art ivory carvings bronzes Persian Faenza and Moorish ware statues brass repoussé work and Oriental embroidery in my possession at the time of my decease.' In addition to all the objets d'art the bequest included 150 oil paintings, watercolours, prints and drawings and 1,700 books.

There are no diaries which might establish the itinerary of Powell's version of the Grand Tour abroad. He carefully preserved his correspondents' letters and had them bound into 11 volumes (he also pasted newspaper cuttings and reviews concerning his own and his friends' activities and those of his musical and literary heroes into a scrapbook entitled *Gleanings*). The letters indicate to a certain degree where he travelled on the continent, but very little is included about how he purchased his collection, only fourteen of his own letters survive, written to Algernon Swinburne and Simeon Solomon, and now in the Brotherton Library, Leeds. Over one hundred letters from the poet Algernon Charles Swinburne (1837-1909) are included in Powell's bound correspondence. The two men became close friends from 1865 onwards, visited each other in London and Aberystwyth and both stayed at Powell's cottage near Etretat, Normandy in 1868. The letters reveal that both shared a fascination with corporal punishment and its literary exegesis in the works of the Marquis de Sade. (Swinburne too had attended Eton.) Powell named his cottage Chaumière Dolmancé after a character in De Sade's *La Philosophie dans le Boudoir* and their adventures there are related by Guy de Maupassant in his story *L'anglais d'Etretat* and also in the Goncourt brothers *Journal* (28.ii.1875). Maupassant met Powell and Swinburne in the summer of 1868 at Etretat when he attempted to rescue Swinburne from the sea. In Maupassant's fictional account Powell appears as a proto-type of J K Huysman's Des Essientes in *Au Rebours*, seeming at first gentle and kind to his visitors but acting in an increasingly bizarre manner, living with a monkey yet rumoured to eat only monkey flesh, possessing an album of pornographic photographs of soldiers, sucking on the fingers of a severed, mummified hand and so on, and of course outraging the locals. In the short story he describes Powell's character: 'He loved the supernatural, the macabre, the tortured, the intricate and every form of derangement'. In the tradition of many eccentric collectors such

J M W Turner (1775-1851) *Folly Bridge, Oxford* watercolour c.1794

Dante Gabriel Rossetti (1828-82)
Ruth Herbert pencil 1858

Simeon Solomon (1840-1905)
Roman Youth watercolour 1869

Edward Burne Jones (1833-98) *Seraph* chalk c.1865

Edward J Poynter (1836-1919) *Head of a Young Woman* watercolour 1860s

as Ludwig II of Bavaria and William Beckford, Powell flirted with the boundaries of acceptable behaviour, but safely ensconced in a cottage in Normandy and on rather a less lavish scale. All that remains as material evidence, apart from the correspondence, are watercolours of Etretat by Wilhelm Kümpel (1822-80) and a lock of Swinburne's hair. A watercolour by J B Zwecker of *Nip* the monkey is now missing.

An undated, bound inventory of the paintings in the University is more specific about Powell's methods of acquisition but not always totally convincing; in it Powell indicates with '+' those works 'executed expressly for me'; those annotated with '#' were 'gifts from the artists' and 'GP' (encircled) indicated those produced 'from my own designs'. But there seems to be an element of wishful thinking; the category '+' includes two drawings in red chalk *Female Head* and *Seraph* by Edward Coley Burne-Jones (1833-1898); these appear to be preparatory studies for his painting *Le Chant d'Amour* (1868-77) now in the Metropolitan Museum of Art, New York. An undated letter from Georgiana Burne-Jones acknowledges Powell's payment in person at their house in Fulham. There are two other very similar studies of the *Seraph* in the Ashmolean and British Museums. A watercolour of the same subject, painted in 1865, was purchased by the Scottish collector William Graham who then commissioned the New York painting; it is unlikely therefore that the two Burne-Jones drawings were 'executed expressly' for Powell and more likely that Powell asked for copies of studies he had already seen.

On the other hand the letters from J B Zwecker, Wilhem Kümpel and Simeon and Rebecca Solomon show that Powell was active in commissioning work to his own taste. His correspondence with the artist Johann Baptiste Zwecker (1814-1876) in particular attests to a close working relationship. Zwecker illustrated Powell and Eiríkur Magnússons' *Legends of Iceland* (First & Second Series, Richard Bentley, 1864-66) and painted many watercolours on this theme for Powell, some of them from Powell's designs. They began their correspondence in 1864 and it continued until Zwecker's death in 1876. Powell encouraged and supported Zwecker throughout the artist's long periods of ill-health. Zwecker was a well-known illustrator whose work appeared regularly in periodicals such as *Good Words* and *Once a Week*; he also illustrated various works on travel and natural history - a number of them by David Livingstone and H M Stanley. His magnum opus was the illustration of the Reverend John George Wood's *Illustrated Natural History* (three volumes, Routledge 1861) and his *Natural History of Man* (five volumes, Routledge 1863-70). Zwecker's replies to Powell's letters from Leipzig, Madrid and Algiers are often decorated in the headings and margins with vignettes of his own dreams and adventures and with portraits of Powell in different guises. In a letter Zwecker describes Powell as 'a Will O'the Wisp, here there, everywhere, nobody can follow... now in Spain, in the twinkle of an eye in Paris again'. (27.ii.1866) Many letters also make reference to the works commissioned by Powell. One describes his painting *The Nautilus - A Dream in Fever*, painted from a specimen Zwecker had bought especially: 'The picture succeeded better than I expected. The colours of the Nautilus and deep, deep blue sea, blend beautifully. I really thank you did give me to do such a bold bit of colouring ... I hope you will send me some new ideas for painting, I shall be delighted to embody them with brush and colour.' (c.May 1865) Powell paid Zwecker, often in advance, anything from five to 30 guineas per work.

His close friend Algernon Swinburne introduced Powell to the young artist Simeon Solomon (1840-1905). From his correspondence it is clear that Powell sometimes suggested ideas for compositions to Solomon. He purchased three watercolours by Solomon who was closely associated with the Pre-Raphaelite circle and later the Aesthetic Movement - *Noon*, *A Roman Youth* and *Love Dreaming by the Sea*; the latter two were both commissioned by Powell. *A Roman Youth* was painted when the artist was in Rome in 1869 where he wrote his prose poem *A Vision of Love Revealed in Sleep*, published in 1871. In an undated letter from Solomon to Powell he consults his patron about the composition: 'would you like the ruined temple background to your "Love" or the sea + sky that we spoke of elsewhere - will you kindly let me have a line as it is being begun'. Solomon's homosexuality earned him notoriety, an eighteen-month suspended sentence and eventual destitution. After Simeon's arrest in 1873 Powell, unlike Swinburne, appears to have kept in contact with the Solomons. *The Wounded Dove* is the only work by Simeon's sister Rebecca Solomon (1832-1886) in the collection; her letters to Powell confirm that she was paid £15 in installments, the last of which was made in 1873. She trained under her brother Abraham and attended Spitalfields School of Design. The work she exhibited between 1850 and 1874 was favourably reviewed and reproduced in contemporary art magazines but after her brother's arrest her promising career came to an abrupt end.

Powell also collected a number of works from the more well-known Pre-Raphaelites - two pencil drawings by Dante Gabriel Rossetti (1828-1882) of *Clara Vaughan Morgan* 1874 and *Ruth Herbert* 1858 and a watercolour of the head of a young woman by Sir Edward Poynter (1836-1919) who eventually became President of the Royal Academy in 1896. Powell placed particular value on *Ruth Herbert*, quoted in the *College Magazine* 1882-83 he writes 'Pictures of this noblest of artist-poets being of such extreme rarity and immense value, it has taken me five years of constant search to find this very interesting specimen' suggesting that the work was not procured directly from the artist. Most of the paintings and drawings of female sitters in Powell's collection are epicine, or ethereal. The watercolours of 'scenes of Spanish life' by P J Antoine are slightly more robust - his *Woman with a Tambourine*, *The Drummer* and *The Fan* are more in the Realist vein but very little is known about him except that he worked and exhibited in London.

Powell also bought paintings which were more of the academic or 'old master' variety, some of them genuine, some copies; these he may have purchased in sale rooms in London possibly through the agency of Mr Gullick from whom there is some correspondence. They include two early watercolours by J M W Turner (1775-1851) *Folly Bridge, Oxford* (c1794) and *Westminster Bridge* (c1796); two landscapes attributed to John Crome (1768-1821); two paintings attributed to John Constable (1776-1837), *Branch Hill Pond, Hampstead Heath* (probably by John Linnell) and *A Country Road* (possibly by F W Watts) and three large watercolours by Richard Westall (1765-1836): *Satan Calling Forth His Legions* (1792), *A Nymph and two Satyrs* and *The Birth of Sin,* all finished studies for engravings illustrating John Boydell's edition of Milton's *Poetical Works* (1792-94).

The paintings and objets d'art also reveal a decided interest in the male nude particularly in the collection of small bronzes. Some are Renaissance, some 18th or 19th-century copies of Renaissance originals and some are contemporary pieces made by well-known sculptors of the time such as *On the sea shore* (1877) (a black woman manacled in slavery) by John Bell (1812-1895), *Pan* by Jean Baptiste Clésinger (1814-1883) and *Bacchus* by Victoriano Codina-Länglin (1844-1911). The overall theme of the bronzes is the male nude in classical guise, subject matter which is echoed in some of Zwecker's watercolours, particularly the overtly phallic *Boy on a Dragonfly, Ajax* by Etienne Garnier and *Love Dreaming by the Sea* by Simeon Solomon. Homoeroticism is undeniably one of the prime organising principles of Powell's collection of fine and decorative art.

As for the other artefacts in the collection there are few clues to where they were acquired: a Liberty's label on a piece of Satsuma pottery, a label from F De Soye of Paris on a Japanese ivory carving; a claim to have found intaglios (carved gemstones) 'between Mayence and Ingelheim during the 1869-70 war' (*UCW Calendar*, 1899-1900; p273) or to have excavated various antiquities, given to the Museum in 1879, 'in ancient tombs in the neighbourhood of the Rhine' and to have collected a series of silver ornaments 'and other articles' during his Icelandic travels. Two Islamic tiles from Antatolia and Persia and a Moroccan bowl he may have picked up on his travels in North Africa or Spain. The paintings by Gustave Guillaumet (1840-1887) and Diaz de la Peña (1807-1876), drawings by Horace Vernet (1789-1863) and Etienne Garnier (1759-1849) and his collection of Limoges enamels may have been acquired in France; the latter include two 'Twelve Caesar' candlesticks and two plaques by Jacques Laudin (c.1627-1695).

Powell was very taken with Romantic struggles for liberty and nationhood. Like many other collectors in the 19th century he collected material associated with Napoleon Bonaparte. He bequeathed two images of the Emperor wrought in minute calligraphy by the imprisoned 'Maestro di Pavia' c.1825; a profile constructed from an account of the battle of Waterloo and a full-length portrait in Imperial robes is simultaneously the text of Napoleon's last will and testament. Powell was also a supporter of the Icelandic nationalist and writer Jón Árnusson, giving him £1,500 ostensibly to write a definitive history of his homeland which was never completed. It was from Árnusson's collection of *Legends of Iceland* (1862-64) that Eiríkur Magnússon and Powell took their selection. There is no evidence to suggest that Powell felt any similar concerns for the fate of the Welsh nation or language.

The natural sciences are also represented in Powell's gifts in the form of 'natural curiosities': specimens of Icelandic rocks and minerals - Iceland spar, malachite, agates, antimony and various ores; fossil specimens from Tremadog and pieces of wood from the submerged forest at Hastings: the rattle of a rattlesnake, a specimen of Lacerta Gouldi and two dried specimens of hippocampus, the molar of an elephant and a piece of organ-pipe coral. The 'artificial curiosities' included many artefacts from Japan: sixteen Japanese netsukes (small carved figures, many of skeletons or skulls) and eight *Kagimabuta* netsukes (rice-cake shaped netsukes with discs of metal incised and appliqued with scenes from Japanese legend); eleven larger ivory *okimono* carvings, some *ojime* (small coral or ivory beads) and five bronze *tsuba* or sword guards; a group of Japanese arrows in a leather stand, a bronze spider crab, an ornate bronze and brass medicine cabinet, a cast iron saki kettle and two enamelled metal vases; other 'curiosities' include a Chinese magician's crystal wand; a large number of 'Oriental and other manuscripts'; old Persian needlework; a pair of Canadian snowshoes and a carved wooden effigy of a New Zealand chief. The European rarities include autograph signatures of Henry III and Henry IV of France; and a Papal Bull of Pope Urban VIII of 1637. The list begins to resemble the contents of a 17th-century *Wünderkammer*.

Powell was a fanatical devotee of Wagner and attended the first performance of the *Ring* cycle. A list, preserved by Powell, of those attending Bayreuth in August 1876 describes Powell as 'Gelehrter' - a learned gentleman or man of letters. By his own account he also had dinner with the 'Great Master' and his wife Cosima in September 1876 (letter to Swinburne 11.ix.1876). The relic of this experience was a dried flower from the gardens at Bayreuth (long since lost). He amassed a number of musical manuscripts and autographs including *Ode upon the New Year* (1693) by Dr John Blow (1649-1708), and Orazio Benecoli's *Dixit Dominus* (1668). In 1862 he purchased from the sale of the library of the Society for British Musicians an autographed manuscript of Mendelssohn's concert overture *Meerestille und glückliche farht (Calm sea and prosperous voyage)* 1832 - the score is an authentic working document by the composer. Powell also bequeathed a plaster-cast of Mendelssohn's hand. There is an element of the souvenir about much of his music memorabilia - and occasionally a suggestion of the relic - the coffee service he thought had belonged to Mozart (but was in fact made by the Gieshübl Porcelain Factory in Bohemia

Rebecca Solomon (1832-1886) *The Wounded Dove* watercolour c.1872

Johann Baptiste Zwecker (1814-1876) *Nautilus - A Dream in Fever* watercolour 1865

Japanese stoneware figure

Victoriano Codina-Länglin (1844-1911)
Bacchus bronze c.1870

German rock crystal and enamelled silver casket
(once containing a fragment of Schumann's coffin)

two decades after Mozart's death in 1791), a Parian bust of Beethoven, a fragment of Robert Schumann's coffin in a beautifully enamelled silver and rock crystal casket (only the casket remains). Powell was acquainted with Schumann's wife, the pianist and composer Clara Schumann. He also bequeathed autograph letters of Schumann, Weber, Cherubini, Hummel and Drs. Blow, Boyce and Croft. His music manuscripts were left to Dr. Joseph Parry's College in Swansea but later returned to Aberystwyth. The artist Wilhelm Kümpel (1822-80) a mutual friend of Powell and Zwecker was commissioned to produce crayon portraits of Powell's musical and literary heroes among them Henry Wadsworth Longfellow, Robert Schumann and Richard Wagner. Powell also bequeathed an engraved portrait of Wagner by Sir Hubert von Herkomer.

Powell's collection was not formed in any systematic fashion, nor is there any evidence to suggest that while it was in his possession it was arranged or displayed in any ordered manner - as a private museum or a secret *studiolo* - to demonstrate any rational point to potential spectators. Most of the objects which Powell gave and bequeathed to the University were part of the decor of his house at 41, Mornington Crescent in north London, little came from Nanteos. Nevertheless, en masse, his collections do constitute Powell's personal Theatre of Memory - they are representative of his personal enthusiasms, they had strong significance as precious souvenirs of friends and relics of heroes, as illustrations of his status as man of letters, a scholar, a benefactor, a patron to young genius and an equal among the great and the good - in his own words his collections were 'the reality of my dreams'. This nostalgic aspect of his collection - artefacts amassed to authenticate Powell's experiences, to summon them but never to recoup them - now colours our picture of Powell. He left no narrative to supplement the artefacts and as they were dispersed throughout the University, their collective meanings suffered concurrent attrition.

Powell's collection also conforms to historical precedents. It contains the material acquired by any 'serious' art collector in the mid-19th century, following the model of Renaissance princely collections; in this instance without the means of a William Beckford (1759-1844) or a George Salting (1836-1909) or the knowledge and connoiseurship of a Charlotte Schrieber (1812-95) or Lord Llangattock (John Rolls). The paintings, objets d'art, curios, souvenirs and relics seen together are imbued with Powell's own slant on the world; separated, unsequenced, dispersed they are dumb; in the canon of art history as moments in a progression they are 'second rate' or 'minor pieces', in the language of the auction house many are 'without provenance', 'attributed', copies or even fakes. But together the artefacts and associated literature are an invaluble resource for the reconstruction of the world view of a 19th-century collector, and the examination through time of our relationship with material goods in collections. **NH**

Shigayaki ware 19th-century Japanese

Jacques Laudin (c.1627-95) *Ignis* 17th-century Limoges enamel

Sastuma ware Japanese early-mid 19th century

Sir John Williams

On his death in 1926, Sir John Williams the internationally renowned Professor of Obstetric Medicine, eminent Court physician and President of the Gynaecologists and Obstetricians of the Empire, bequeathed his house, its contents and one half of his money to the University. The other half, along with pictures relating to Wales, he left to the National Library to join his earlier gift of an outstanding collection of rare books and early Welsh manuscripts. The third son of tenant farmers, Williams lived and worked for most of his career in London, but he never lost sight of his humble origins in rural Carmarthenshire. He remained passionate about all things Welsh and was a generous benefactor of Welsh causes.

John Williams (1840-1926) trained at University College Hospital London, working at the Great Ormond Street and Brompton Hospitals before moving to Swansea as a general practitioner. Here he first began to indulge himself in the passion that was to absorb him for the rest of his life; collecting books and manuscripts. In early 1872 he was appointed to UCH, and in April he married Mary Elisabeth Ann Hughes ("Lizzie") - the only child of Richard Hughes, a managing partner in the Glandwr Tinplate Works at Ynystawe. The couple lived in Harley Street and enjoyed a comfortable life-style taking holidays abroad - they cruised the West Indies in 1881. They bought expensive period furniture, pictures and ceramics according to their taste for eighteenth-century furniture by, or in the style of, Chippendale, Hepplewhite and Sheraton.

In 1883 Williams was promoted to Obstetric Physician and in the following year moved to Queen Anne Street. He became a close friend of the Swansea-born painter, art critic and collector John Deffett Francis (1815-1901). On his advice Williams purchased works of art. Deffett Francis had achieved little success as a portrait painter - though he moved in Bohemian circles and his sitters included Queen Victoria. A founder of the Savage Club he was a friend of Dickens and Ruskin. He returned to Swansea in 1876 and founded the art library and gallery to which he donated many works of art. (He bequeathed almost 20,000 books, prints and drawings to the British Museum.) He dedicated the Catalogue Supplement to John Williams in 1896, 'Of all Welshmen I have known', he wrote, 'no one has been possessed with a keener desire than your own to aid his Countryman's intellectual advancement'.

Rembrandt van Rijn [workshop of] (1606-69) *Christ and the Woman of Samaria* oil 1650s

Deffett Francis sought out paintings that he knew would interest Williams and for this he received financial reward. Williams not only purchased paintings and objet d'art but also received them as gifts from appreciative patients. A cup from Princess Maud 'in remembrance of our small son, whom you helped into the world, and we shall *never* forget your *great* kindness to us' (Letter M to JW, 15.x.1903) and rare items of Aztec pottery from H G Stevens of Regent Street with a note 'I am feeling much better thanks to your kind attention for which I am very much obliged.' (Undated letter from HGS to JW) In 1898 Deffett Francis gave several paintings 'with fervent gratitude to you and your Lady', amongst these one labelled 'Sir Joshua's study for the Colour of his Portrait of the Duke of Orleans - the picture was painted for the Prince of Wales but was destroyed by fire. This study did belong to H Thompson RA who worked for Sir J. R.' and 'A sketch by Gericault for his large picture of "The Death of Herules" in the Louvre'. (Letter to JW from JDF, 27.ix.1898)

Deffett Francis was not the most discriminating or discerning of collector-dealers. Over zealous in his attribution of paintings both for himself and for John Williams many have now been relegated to the rank 'School of ...' or 'Follower of ...'. Amongst Williams' oil paintings are works once ascribed to Rembrandt, Rosa, Watteau, Gericault and Reynolds. *An Eruption of Vesuvius, seen from Portici* 1774-6 by Joseph Wright of Derby (1734-1797) is arguably the artist's most impressive and successful painting of the subject, but there is no documentation to connect its acquisition to Deffett Francis. Amongst the watercolours and prints is a volume, inscribed by Deffett Francis, of some 198 wash drawings by the Italian painter Tommaso Minardi (1787-1871) - the only known volume outside of Italy.

Jean-Baptiste Deshays or ?Charles-Michelange Challe [formerly attributed to Gericault] *Death of Hercules* oil 1810s

In 1886 Williams was asked by Queen Victoria to attend to Princess Beatrice who was expecting a child. She was the first of many Royals to whom he became medical advisor - a service for which he received a Baronetcy in 1894. Now at the height of his career and a more confident, experienced collector, he purchased entire private libraries. In 1899 he bought from the Earl of Macclesfield the unique collection formed by Rev. Samuel Williams in the late seventeenth century. It included *The Red Book of Talgarth* (1400). In 1905 he purchased the Hengwrt-Peniarth collection, formed by Robert Vaughan also in the seventeenth century. It included the earliest known manuscript in Welsh *The Black Book of Carmarthen*, the earliest complete manuscript of the Mabinogion *The White Book of Rhydderch* and *The Book of Taliesin* (c.1275).

On retirement in 1903 Sir John and Lady Williams returned to Wales leasing the Plas at Llanstephen where he became Justice of the Peace and High Sheriff of Carmarthenshire. He now channelled his energies into a cause very dear to him, leading the campaign to establish a National Library of Wales; a government-supported institution to house books, manuscripts and artefacts concerning the history of Wales, its literature and its people. Thirteen acres of the Penglais estate at Aberystwyth were acquired for the Library from Lord Rendel, President of the University. Meanwhile, Cardiff and Swansea both made

Sir John Williams c.1900

Joshua Reynolds (1723-92) [after] *Philippe Egalite, Duc d'Orleans*
oil 1790s

claims to be the most appropriate location for the Library. However, state support was dependent upon local contributions and gifts and John Williams held the trump card, his magnificent personal library - 1,200 manuscripts and some 25,000 volumes - which he promised to the Nation *only* if the Library were to be situated in Aberystwyth. Eventually the hard fought battle to secure the Library for Aberystwyth was won with the support of Rendel and David Davies of Llandinam. Sir John was appointed its first President and Sidney Kyffin Greenslade engaged as architect.

It was not long after his books were transferred to Aberystwyth that Lord and Lady Williams moved there themselves, to a house on the promenade, renaming it Blaenllynant after his parents' farm. He played an active role in the Library and in 1913 he succeeded Rendel as President of the

Tommaso Minardi (1787-1871) *'Two women and a babe in arms'*
ink and wash 1850s

University, a position he held until his death. Lady Williams died in 1915 just months after she presented her collection of early 19th-century Swansea and Nantgarw porcelain to the University. 'A valuable collection', wrote H J Fleure in the *Annual Reports* for 1915, 'illustrating a Welsh artistic industry, and this fills a great lacuna in the Museum which aims at illustrating human effort in such a way as to encourage students to take more serious interest in their own country, its traditions and its artistic efforts'.

After Williams' death in 1926 the University sold Blaenllynant and its contents were distributed around halls of residence, offices and the Museum. Lesser items, including engravings after French and English paintings were sold. The important Queen Anne and Georgian furniture - from the salon, library, dining room and bedrooms - have since graced the Principal's official residence. Williams was foremost a bibliophile and his library of Welsh books and manuscripts was systematically acquired. The group of paintings however were never concieved as a collection, no apparent rationale underpins his acquisition of works of art. Not surprisingly there are Welsh subjects but for the most part, the oil paintings were purchased for their decorative qualities, to complement his eighteenth century furniture. **RM**

Swansea and Nantgarw china 19th century

the Gallery of Crafts 1918-1962

In the 1910s there was an increasing concern for the state of the visual arts in Wales. In 1918 a *Report on the Teaching of Art in the Intermediate Schools of Wales* by painter, etcher and art educationalist Frederick Charles Richards (1878-1932) stated that 'in our universities from among 641 degrees there is not one degree in Fine Art'. Soon afterwards the University of Wales set up an arts committee and it is likely that through his friendship with fellow Welshman Dr Thomas Jones, and in turn Jones' friendship with Gwendoline and Margaret Davies, Richards was instrumental in persuading Aberystwyth to establish the Art and Crafts Department and Museum in 1918. Gwendoline Davies had already written to Professor Fleure in 1916 asking if there had been any progress in developing the teaching of art at the University. (MV:1980, p.43)

In the years 1917-1920 the Davies sisters were also considering the possibility of setting up a craft centre at Gregynog. Gwendoline Margaret (1882-1951) and her sister Margaret Sydney (1884-1963) were the grand-daughters of David Davies 'Top Sawyer', the Victorian entrepreneur and industrialist who amassed a great fortune from mining, shipping and the railways in south Wales. At the turn of the century the sisters inherited a large part of his wealth which they used in generous support of art, music, literature, education, religion, politics, welfare and health affairs in Wales. They purchased Gregynog Hall, near Newtown, Montgomeryshire with their brother in 1914, buying out his share in 1920 to turn the house into a rural centre for Art and Crafts for the rehabilitation of soldiers and those affected by the war. Their dream was never fully realised but the fine books produced by Gregynog Press between 1923 and 1940 won international acclaim. In 1924 Gregynog became the home of the sisters and their renowned collection of French 19th-century art which they bequeathed to the National Museum of Wales in Cardiff.

Gwendoline and Margaret had met Thomas Jones ('TJ') in 1910 with their brother, the first Lord Davies. Jones became their closest friend and confidant. As Secretary to the Cabinet, Jones served under four Prime Ministers and he was well connected within Wales. After graduating from Aberystwyth he moved to Glasgow and there came into contact with the work of Charles Rennie Macintosh. He and his wife filled their home with the fruits of good 'honest craftsmanship' - with hand-made furniture, silver, enamels and pottery. 'TJ' was an Arts and Crafts devotee in the William Morris manner and he was pivotal in the sisters' plans for Aberystwyth and Gregynog.

The teaching of art at Aberystwyth began in the late 19th century with the activities of the Drawing Master and other manual teachers engaged by the Department of Education for the training of elementary and secondary school teachers. Around 1917 the sub-Department of Art and Crafts emerged as a discrete part of the Department of Education. Daniel Rowland Jones (1875-1934) who was formerly craft instructor at summer schools in Aberystwyth, and art master at Ardwyn Grammar School, became full-time Drawing Master. He was assisted by Valerius de Saedeleer (1867-1941) and his daughters who were among the group of Belgian refugee artists brought to Wales by the Davies sisters in September 1914.

Another kindred spirit was Professor Fleure who was also an Arts and Crafts enthusiast. Since 1910 he had set out to give ' a sketch of human workmanship in periods and regions ... to work up to a collection of fine modern workmanship'. In September 1916 he wrote to TJ 'we could develop a growing organisation for promoting arts and crafts and music'. (MV:1980, p.42) Jones and Fleure persuaded the Davies sisters that there was a need for a teaching collection for students to appreciate contemporary British art and craft at first hand. In 1918 they gave £5,000 as an endowment fund 'to provide income for the museum's needs'. The Gregynog venture and Aberystwyth's collection would, it was hoped, lead to an arts and crafts revival in Wales. The aim was to instruct and inspire trainee teachers to carry on the good work in schools - especially local schools, which would in turn foster revivals in local craft industries.

In 1918, on the recommendation of Thomas Jones, the sisters invited his friend the architect Sidney Kyffin Greenslade (1866-1955) to become 'Consulting Curator' to the Art and Crafts Museum. Greenslade was still working on the building of the National Library of Wales; his designs had won the competition in 1909. He had also designed TJ's house for him at Thanet. A native of Exeter, and the son the Chief Clerk of the Probate Court, Greenslade had sufficient private means to pursue his love of art and crafts. A collector of pottery, prints, fine books and glass himself, Greenslade was recognised by his contemporaries as an authority on the history of British ceramics and an expert on the Martin Brothers. Sharing his time between Exeter and his rooms in London at 11 Gray's Inn Square, Greenslade visited private galleries, society exhibitions, artists' studios

Graham Sutherland (1903-80) *The Philosophers* etching 1924

Celadon glaze mallet vase and incense burner

The first invoice to the Gallery of Crafts 1920

Lao-tzu Japanese bronze incense burner

Graham Sutherland (1903-80) *Evening, the Black Rabbit/Chalkpit on the Arun* watercolour 1924

F H Spear *Circus Horses* lithograph 1933

West African baskets, cowrie shell

and antique shops with an annual budget in the vicinity of £250, acquiring crafts for the University; prints, ceramics, glass, basket work, calligraphy, private press books and ethnographic material. Old and new were bought so that the two might be compared.

It was not long before the Gallery became overcrowded and there was an urgent need to rationalise the collections. In 1924 scientific specimens were distributed to departments and the General Museum was re-named the Gallery of Crafts. The Gallery was opened to the public, and on occasions Greenslade made himself available to give tours. TJ recounts to his wife an occasion when Greenslade talked on the Aberystwyth collections when on loan to Coleg Harlech in 1932: 'S K Greenslade, inimitable, brilliant, for about forty minutes, humorous, serious, passionate, 'wonderful' and 'astounding' - people thrilled by him - a real treat. He began with prehistoric adzes and bowls and came down to Cardew and Leach'. (TJ:1954, p.66)

Sidney Kyffin Greenslade (1866-1955)

Dan Jones who had taken responsibility for the formation of a Welsh Folk Craft collection, became Curator of the Museum in 1924. The collections were at the core of teaching; Oxford classical scholar Principal Sir Henry Stuart-Jones lectured on 'Greek and Roman Life and Art', Dan Jones on 'Welsh Craftsmanship', and H J Fleure on 'Art and Primitive Life'. In 1933 the inclusion of art and crafts courses at the Intermediate and Subsidiary levels of the BA degree was approved. It was also recognised that whilst most of the art and crafts activities were undertaken on behalf of the Education Department, a great deal had taken place outside of that Department. In July 1933, Council agreed that the Department of Art and Crafts and its staff become entirely independent of the Education Department and that Dan Jones be recognised as Head of the Department. Jones appointed Robert Lambert Gapper bsc arca as temporary assistant lecturer in 1934.

The Department's autonomy was all too short lived, Gapper was soon to be carving the memorial stone for Dan Jones who died suddenly during the Michaelmas term that year. In the *Annual Reports* (1935) Professor C R Chapple mourned 'a man of single-minded devotion to his work ... The development of Art in this College has not corresponded to his wishes, but its progress from the use of a few blackboards in the Examination Hall to a recognised University subject is some measure of the energy and devotion which Mr Jones gave to his task'. In that short time Principal Henry Stuart-Jones, who had always been a very keen supporter of the art department, was succeeded by Ifor L Evans. At a special meeting of Council following Jones' death it was decided to curtail the activities of the Art and Crafts Department and Gallery. Evans wrote in a memorandum 'Art at Aberystwyth' (17.iv.1944) that it was his view that fine and allied arts were best left to the Schools of Art. 'By their very nature, these subjects can hardly form part of a normal academic curriculum as represented by a course of study for an initial degree ... There would seem to be no place for art at Aberystwyth'. Evans persuaded the Davies sisters to allow him to re-direct all but £1,000 of the original museum gift for a new Agricultural Science building and Greenslade was dismissed.

The sisters by now were very disillusioned with the University for which they once had such great hopes. Disappointment started when TJ was unsuccessful in his application for Principalship in 1920 and there was further dismay as they witnessed their plans for a thriving Art and Crafts Department never properly materialise. H J Fleure left for Manchester after 'ten desolate years fighting parochial attitudes in Aberystwyth' and with him went the political clout and the only strong voice for the Arts and Crafts cause within the University. (MV:1980, p.49) By the time Lambert Gapper took responsibility for the teaching of art and the mantle of curatorship the odds were heavily stacked against him.

In 1936 the University was experiencing a crisis of accommodation and space was created in the Gallery for committee tables. The transition between the room's use as museum and committee room was very gradual. In 1943 all the museum objects were finally packed away to the basement providing temporary accommodation for the RAF classes. The cases of exhibits were reinstated after two years; by 1946 two-thirds of the collection was back on display, and by 1949 all that was previously on display had been returned. In 1952 Lambert Gapper recalled for display all the small oil paintings and most of the prints. He believed strongly in the collection's worth as a teaching resource, it is 'the "backbone" of the Art Department', he wrote in a letter to Professor of Education Idwal Jones, 'It is evident that any instruction and appreciation in Art must be reinforced by the presence of actual works of art ... and so my aim is to build up and enrich the present collection as a means of profounder study'. (19.i.1950) His appeal passed unheeded, in 1955 the Gallery was requisitioned once more for meetings - ceramics were moved to corridors and store cupboards, and the prints and paintings were sent out to halls of residence and staff common rooms. The erosion of the Gallery of Crafts continued until only the Welsh wooden artefacts remained, they too were banished in 1959 to allow for the refurbishment of the room to form the Council Chamber. In that year the teaching facilities for Art moved to the Cambrian Street premises and Gapper had the museum cases re-erected there. In 1960 he reported that 'most of the artefacts' were back on display. Lambert Gapper retired in 1962 and the curatorship passed to his successor David Tinker. **RM**

Prints of the Inter-War Years

Samuel Palmer (1805-81) *The Bellman* etching 1879

By the end of the 19th century attitudes towards etching had changed significantly, principally through the endeavours of James McNeill Whistler (1834-1903) who helped establish the notion of the limited edition fine art print. As a consequence etching attained respectability as an art form in its own right, free from its illustrative and reproductive origins. The so-called 'Etching Revival' culminated in the 1920s with an unprecedented market for contemporary prints - modern etchings were highly prized, affordable and a symbol of good taste. The high demand for etchings and the promise of commercial success turned many young artists to printmaking.

In his acquisition of prints Greenslade neither set out to illustrate the entire history of printmaking nor the development of the modern fine art print since Whistler. He purchased prints (largely etchings), and ceramics, mainly by contemporary practitioners to demonstrate 'very simple and unaffected work by acknowledged masters of their Art'. (*Annual Reports* 1925) Greenslade who was an acclaimed authority on ceramics, was not so well versed in contemporary printmaking - he certainly did not have access to the same influential network of galleries, curators, dealers, collectors and artists as he did with ceramics. At times his choice of prints can appear indiscriminate. The subject matter is as varied as the artists represented - views of castles and ruins, agrarian landscapes and rural pursuits, flora and fauna, portraits and figure compositions but few scenes dealing with contemporary life. Between November 1921 and April 1935 he purchased prints directly from the artists, art schools, and from London galleries and publishers such as Beaux Arts, Colnaghi's and the 21 Gallery. He paid between two and five guineas for any one print with a six guinea ceiling established in May 1922 for F L Griggs' *Minsden Episcopi*. He matched this figure on five subsequent occasions but he did not break the ceiling until April 1931 when he paid £6-16-0 to Joseph Webb for *The Rat Barn*. The most he was eventually to pay was seven guineas for Webb's *Chepstow from the Cliff* at Colnaghi's in 1933.

Paul Drury (1903-87) *After Work* etching 1926

Many young printmakers are represented in the collection - the artists' eventual place in art history or the investment value of their prints did not concern him. Graham Sutherland was still a student at Goldsmiths' College of Art and about to embark upon a professional career when Greenslade purchased eight etchings and a watercolour from his first one-man show in the 21 Gallery in October 1924. Edgar Holloway was just seventeen when he etched the self portrait bought from the same gallery, and Mabel Annesley, Celia Fiennes and Rosa Hope were students at Central School of Art and Crafts when they sold prints directly to Greenslade. The high standards set by London art students were to provide students at Aberystwyth with realistic and attainable goals. A course in etching had been introduced in 1920 and it was hoped students would improve their design, execution and techniques 'due to careful study of and the good influence of the collections.' (*Annual Reports*, 1925)

Graham Sutherland (1903-80) *Pecken Wood* etching 1925

F L Griggs (1876-1938) *Sellinger* etching 1917

Joseph Webb (1908-62) *Asylum* etching 1930-1

Greenslade reflected popular middle-class taste for the 'traditional' etchers. His endeavour to illustrate good craftsmanship led inevitably to the exclusion of modernist concerns in contemporary printmaking in which artistic statement and expression assumed greater importance than skill and craftsmanship. For example, there are no works by avant-garde exponents such as Paul Nash, C R W Nevinson, Edward Wadsworth or the Vorticist linocuts of Claude Flight and his students at the Grosvenor School. Greenslade preferred the work from craft-orientated courses at Central and Goldsmiths' schools rather than the Royal College of Art, which through Sir Frank Short had been the mainstay of the Whistlerian etched line. There was no place for prints by Whistler and his followers (James McBey, D Y Cameron or even Augustus John) in Greenslade's scheme of things. Generally prints by these artists were prohibitively expensive for Greenslade, on occasion realising hundreds of pounds at the London sale rooms.

Whistler's departure from naturalistic representation, his spontaneous and impressionistic treatment of form and 'creative' wiping of the plates for atmospheric effect did not impress Greenslade. Furthermore, Whistler's flashy showmanship did not conform to his idea of 'simple and unaffected' craft. The nearest he came to the Whistlerian idiom (and the *Thames Set* 1860 in particular), was in the delicate and stylish prints of Thomas Jones's friend, the etcher Fred Richards who was teaching at the RCA where he had earlier trained under Frank Short. In addition to purchases made by the Museum, Thomas Jones gave six etchings personally inscribed to him (four of Venice and two of Egypt) to the University in 1947. There are no etchings comparable to Richards' in the collection but there is a particularly undistinguished group of 14 etchings by Edgar Wilson (1861-1918) most of which attempt to emulate Whistlerian river scenes. These were purchased by Greenslade at regular intervals from November 1921 to April 1934.

The overall tone of the inter-war prints in the collection is conservative and for the most part backward looking - to a past golden age, an idyll or sanctuary of rural life which was deemed to be under threat. This aspect of the print market between the wars is represented

Edgar Holloway (b.1914) *Self Portrait No.6* etching 1932

Edward Bouverie Hoyton (1900-88) *Head of a Jew* etching 1925

by a group of etchers who were contemporaries at Goldsmiths' School of Art in the mid 1920s: Graham Sutherland (1903-1980), Paul Drury (1903-87), Edward Bouverie Hoyton (1900-88) and William Larkins (1901-74). Their vision of rural Britain was partly derived from the renewed interest in the Shoreham drawings and late etchings of Samuel Palmer (1805-81), and from the etchings and mentorship of Frederick Landseer Griggs (1876-1938) - who reprinted the Palmer etchings in the collection.

F L Griggs' etchings of monumental Gothic cathedrals and visionary scenes of medieval England displayed sentiments akin to Sutherland's own. In 1925 Sutherland and Drury made a pilgrimage to stay with Griggs at Chipping Camden where he played a significant role in the arts and crafts community. He demonstrated wiping and printing techniques to the young students and imparted his enthusiasm for the emotional power of Palmer's work. In fact, the first prints bought for the collection by Greenslade (from the 21 Gallery in November 1921) were six working states of etchings by Griggs - *Mortmain*, *Sellenger*, *Totterne Inn* and *Palace*, *Priory* and *Maur's Farm's* (six more were bought over the next three years). It is interesting to see Palmer's warmth give way to austerity in the haunting atmosphere that pervades Griggs' imaginary old buildings.

The Graham Sutherland etchings purchased in 1924 demonstrate the customary practice for young art students to visit the print rooms of the British Museum and the V&A to learn from the examination of past exponents of their craft. Before his discovery of Palmer, Sutherland's search for a style and subject matter during 1924 took him in many directions from the Düreresque exactitude of *Number 49*, and the plein-air landscape of *The Sluice Gate, Arundel* after the 17-century Dutch etcher van Ostade, to three Rembrantesque etchings made for his unsuccessful application for the Prix de Rome that year - *Cain and Abel*, *Adam and Eve* and *The Philosophers*, the latter is the only proof of the first state. Sutherland's *Pecken Wood* and *Village*, purchased in September 1925, are typical of the depictions of rural or agrarian work by Goldsmiths' students. The small densely-worked plates are heavy with symbolism; thatched cottages, country churches, white doves, the evening star and crescent moon, stooks of corn and men working the fields with a harrow and plough evoke the spirit of autumnal harvest set in anachronistic landscapes of a rural England that no longer existed.

Greenslade also bought three etchings by Palmer from the Cotswold Gallery to begin a 'retrospective' collection. Such prints were systematically acquired to demonstrate interrelationships - showing not only how artists could learn from the technique and borrow iconography, but in this case observation becomes secondary to the conveying of religious and spiritual ideals. The landscape was a vehicle for emotions, its physical appearance transformed. Paul Drury's work was for a few years stylistically very similar to Sutherland. *Nicol's Farm* (1925) and *After Work* (1926) bought from the 21 Gallery are among the best of the pastoral tradition, so too are etchings such as Bouverie Hoyton's *Great Seaside Farm* (1926) purchased from the Fine Art Society in 1926 and Stanley R Badmin's *Fallen Mill Sails* (1931) from the 21 Gallery in 1931.

Joseph Webb (1908-1962), in his tender handling of *The Shepherd's Haven* (1929), comes closest to the deeply religious spirit of the Goldsmiths' etchers. More typical, however, are his fantastic ecclesiastical buildings and imagined medieval barns set in haunting landscapes - nearer in fact to F L Griggs but much more emotionally charged. Greenslade amassed for Aberystwyth the largest public collection of Webb's etchings. In conversation with Thomas Jones in 1933 he recalled seeing *Sunrise, Lincoln* at the Royal Society of Painter-Etchers and Engravers (RSPEE) show that year '... and no red star on it, and much the most remarkable thing in the room. Of course, Joseph Webb's mad; he lives in Harrow; he's got his knife in the dealers; I've bought ten of his things; what was I to do? I went up to the Secretary and he said "Of course you'll buy that" - and I did'. (TJ:1954, p.90)

Another strain of the British landscape tradition is evident in the picturesque topographical landscapes and architectural subjects best represented by the drypoints of Kenneth Steel (1906-70), of *Edinburgh Castle* and *Stirling Castle* 1933, and the very factual and precise engravings of Henry Rushbury (1889-1968), *Santa Croce* and *The Walls of Siena* 1922. Greenslade admired painstaking technique and this is nowhere more evident than in the prints of several artists working independently of each other, who interpreted classical subject matter and revived an interest in line engraving. In much the same way that the Goldsmiths' etchers drew upon the past, both the process of line engraving and classical subject matter allied the artist with the western academic tradition. William E C Morgan (1903-79) was Prix de Rome winner in 1924, beating the other finalists Sutherland and Bouverie Hoyton. Greenslade first encountered Morgan's work at his exhibition in October 1928 at the Beaux Arts Gallery. He purchased four wood-engravings and a self-portrait drawing, and from the 21 Gallery in May 1931 four copper-plate engravings including The Brook (1929) and his masterpiece *Perseus* (1929).

The young *Perseus* seated in triumph with the decapitated Medusa's head at his feet, flaunts a perfectly proportioned classic physique which now seems rather camp. The 'antique' often provided a vehicle for nudity in engraving but this was seldom the case in

Nathaniel Sparks (1880-1957)
Adam line engraving 1931

William E C Morgan (1903-79) *Perseus* line engraving 1929

contemporary etching. The closely engraved lines and the overall attention to details is very Germanic in execution. There are also distinct echoes of Dürer in the engraving of *Adam* (1931) by Nathaniel Sparks (1880-1957) in which Death visits the effete young Adam to remind him of the transience of human life. This *tour de force*, purchased from the RSPEE in 1931, was a memorial plate to Henry Hardy (brother of Thomas, both cousins to Sparks). The figure of Adam has been copied and reversed from Durer's engraving of *Adam and Eve* (1504). By contrast, *The Coursers* (1931) is a more animated subject by Harry Morley (1881-1943) who was a student of Robert Austin (1895-1973) at the Royal College of Art. *The Sisters of Assisi* (1925) and *Litany* (1935) by Austin show the influence of Italian Primitives of the Quattrocento. Unlike *Perseus* which is congested with detail, areas of the plate are left unworked.

Historically, the precision of engraving and etching has lent itself to portraiture and self-portraiture with a long tradition that spanned from Rembrandt and van Dyck to Augustus John. In the 1920s, Gerald Brockhurst's finely crafted etchings were the most sought after, and he was a special favourite of Studio magazine who admired his 'depth of insight all too rare in these days of hasty painting and shallow emotions'. The price of Brockhurst etchings rose quickly beyond Greenslade's ceiling price and he was unable to afford the more highly prized portraits of Brockhurst's dewy-eyed wife Anaïs or his model and mistress Dorette. However, the monumental *Almina* (1924), the sensuous, lightly-sketched *Study for Decoration* (1924) and the intimate portrait of *Najeda* the ballerina (1924) were sufficient to demonstrate the artist's very considerable range. The particularly arresting portraits, *Head of a Jew* and *Head of a Model* by Bouverie Hoyton, purchased in 1925 and 1926 respectively, illustrate a more forthright treatment of facial expression and character. Edgar Holloway (b.1914), who started etching after the print market had peaked, is represented by the third and fifth (final) states of his carefully observed *Self Portrait No.6* (1932) which had been etched under the guidance of Joseph Webb. (More than one 'state' of the same etching was also bought from Griggs and Webb to demonstrate different stages in the development of the image.)

Woodcuts, wood engravings and lithographs are not represented with the same consistency as intaglio prints throughout the period. Molly Bernard Smith, the proprietor of the 21 Gallery who helped so many young etchers at the start their career, was also Secretary of the Senefelder Club, founded in 1908 for the promotion of fine art lithography. From 1920 she hosted their annual exhibitions at the 21 Gallery. The University's one-guinea annual subscription for lay membership starting in 1925 entitled the Art and Crafts Gallery to receive one subscription print by a Club member each year. This set of prints includes some of the most avant-garde examples of contemporary printmaking to find their way into the collection: Gerald Spencer-Pryse (1882-1956, of Plas Gogerddan) *Boardship*, James Fitton *May Day* (1928), Celia Bedford *French Fisherwomen* (1930), F H Spear *Circus Horses* (1933) and W F Colley *The Bull* (1936). **RM**

Harry Morley (1881-1943) *The Coursers* line engraving 1931

Illustrators of the 1860s

John Everett Millais (1829-96) *The Lost Piece of Silver* wood engraving from *Good Words* 1863

On 5th March 1924 Greenslade purchased, at Puttick and Simpson Auctioneers, Leicester Square, fifty boxes of wood-engraved illustrations from Victorian periodicals. The 4,957 prints, for which he paid £8-5-0, had been systematically removed from the leading illustrated magazines of the 'Eighteen Sixties'. It is not known who originally amassed this impressive collection, or who carefully cut them out and hand printed on each the artist's name, its title and source. We do know however that it was a popular pastime amongst Victorian women to save such prints. In his chapter 'The New Appreciation and the New Collector' in *English Illustration - the Sixties 1855-70* published in 1897, Gleeson White described the exact same method of storage and display adopted by the original collector; to fill cloth-covered boxes with sheets of card attaching a print to each and ordering alphabetically by artist. On its arrival in Aberystwyth, the task of cataloguing the collection fell upon Mrs Dan Jones (d.1958) which, according to the *Annual Reports*, she undertook over the next two years.

During the first half of the nineteenth century social and technological developments saw the rapid expansion of the printing industry and the commercial book trade. This was complemented by an enormous demand for illustrated books and magazines. By the 1830s wood engraving, developed in Britain by Thomas Bewick in the 1790s, was firmly established as the cheapest and most successful means of printing an illustration alongside the text. The first magazine to make use of wood engraving as illustration was *The Penny Magazine* in 1832. Punch was established in 1841 and in the following year *The Illustrated London News* first appeared. Large workshops or ateliers were soon established for the production of magazine and book illustrations, most notably the firms of Dalziel, Linton and Swain. The demand for illustrators was initially met by anonymous artists, but the business was soon to attract already established painters, eager to have their work engraved and reach a wider audience. The most significant development in the illustrated magazine came in 1859 with the first of many weeklies that were to flourish during the 1860s. *Once a Week* produced by the proprietors of Punch contained an illustrated miscellany of literature, art, science and popular information. Followed in 1860 by rival magazines, *Good Words* and *The Cornhill*, all three led the way for successive magazines with their illustrations by prominent artists.

Frederick Sandys (1829-1904) *Rosamund, Queen of the Lombards* wood engraving from *Once a Week* 1861

This prolific and important period in the history of British book illustration was in fact a genre or school of illustrators spanning 1855-1875 rather than the decade from which it takes its name. Since the majority of illustrations of the 'sixties appeared in periodicals and not in books the Aberystwyth collection is representative of the illustrative output of the period; indeed some artists are represented by several hundred examples of their work. The majority of prints have been gleaned from the three market leaders, *Once a Week*, *Cornhill* and *Good Words*, whilst *Argosy, Leisure Hour, Sunday at Home* and *The Quiver* are amongst the many other lesser periodicals represented. A large proportion of the collection comprises the work of the 'Realist' school of whom John Everett Millais was the most influential exponent. He is represented by hundreds of prints ranging from his powerful designs for *The Parables of our Lord* (1862) and 'The Bishop and the Knight' (1861) to the sentimentality of 'Polly' (*Good Words* 1864) having forsaken the Pre-Raphaelite exactitude of his earlier work. Other realists include George Pinwell, Whistler, du Maurier, Fred Walker, William Small, Luke Fildes and Herkomer, the humourists John Leech, Charles Keene, Richard Doyle, Kenny Meadows and 'Phiz', and numerous examples by the many women who found an outlet for their work in the periodicals; Helen Allingham, Mary Ellen Edwards and Emily Osbourne among them. Perhaps the most impressive engravings however are those after designs by the Pre-Raphaelites and their successors - Holman Hunt, Burne-Jones, Frederick Sandys, Lord Leighton, Arthur Hughes, Walter Crane and Simeon Solomon.

Literature is represented in the collection by the illustrations to serialised novels of Eliot, Macaulay, Thackeray and Trollope which range from medieval pastiches of courtly love to more potent, melodramatic scenes illustrating the contemporary preoccupation with unrequited love, sickness and death. In addition to their art historical interest, these illustrations are important historical documents, providing an invaluable source of reference to the many facets of Victorian society, reflecting the tastes and aspirations of the new urban reader. From 1936 the Museum was gradually wound down and many of the items were placed in store. After the war two-thirds went on display again but the rest lay forgotten. It was not until 1977 that the wood-engravings, perfectly wrapped and in pristine condition, were discovered in a disused lift-shaft opposite the former Museum in Old College. Since it is still possible to buy odd volumes of the periodicals for only a few pounds, the prints are of no great individual value. However, the fact that they have been mounted and catalogued must surely make them a unique collection. The British Museum has a collection of most of the proofs but the very accessibility and convenience of the Aberystwyth collection makes them invaluable for research without recourse to a multitude of bound volumes. **RM**

Mary Ellen Edwards (1839-1910) *Dressed for a Picnic* wood engraving from *London Society* 1871

Allen W Seaby (1867-1953) *Yellow Hammer and Blackthorn* woodcut c.1933

Yoshijiro Urushibara (1888-1953) *Anemones and Frescias* woodcut c.1928

Colour Woodcuts

The British colour woodcut prints in the collection are a western adaptation of the Japanese *Ukiyo-e* prints of the nineteenth-century and in particular the work of Hokusai (1760-1849) and Hiroshige (1797-1858). They constitute a strand of the 'aesthetic dialogue' between Japan and the West which is in many ways similar to the collaboration between Japanese potters, Bernard Leach and the other British pioneer studio potters. Both potters and printmakers investigated and adapted the methods and philosophies of Japanese art and crafts in their own work, and both sought to learn from and exchange ideas with Japanese artists. Part and parcel of the ethos of the colour woodcut for both collector and artist was the method of production - the skill and precision it demanded and the authentic connection this forged with its Japanese antecedents.

The initial interest in the colour woodcut process in Britain was partly a manifestation of the general 19th-century preoccupation with *Japonisme* and partly stimulated by the Arts and Crafts revival of woodcut printmaking, notably Lucien Pissaro's colour woodcuts for his Eragny Press (1894-1914) and William Nicholson's coloured woodcuts for *Twelve Portraits* (1898). The first attempts to produce colour prints in the Japanese manner, were made by John Dickson Batten (1860-1932), a painter and illustrator who had studied at the Slade School under Alphonse Legros. In 1897 he teamed up with Frank Morley Fletcher (1866-1949), then Professor of Art at University College Reading (1896-1908), and together they developed a technique adapted from a pamphlet *Japanese Wood-Cutting and Wood Printing* by T Tokuno (Smithsonian Institute, Washington 1892).

As in Japan cherry or pear wood was favoured; the plank was dense enough to facilitate delicate work yet soft enough to cut without too much effort. The prints were printed by hand using water-based inks made from finely-ground pigments mixed with water and rice paste brushed onto the block. A separate woodblock was used for each colour, although colours could be blended together on the same block. The blocks were printed on to sized and dampened Japanese mulberry-bark paper using a burnisher or 'barren'. Unlike the Japanese *Ukiyo-e* print which was produced in a workshop in which each step of the process was delegated to a highly specialised worker, the design, cutting and printing of the western colour woodcut was nearly always the work of a single artist.

The resultant technical manual by Morley Fletcher *Wood-block Printmaking: a description of the craft of wood-cutting and colour printing based on the Japanese practice* (James Hobb, 1916) proved to be very influential in the rise in popularity of the medium. He acknowledged Allen William Seaby (1867-1953) as a friend and colleague. Seaby had studied under Fletcher at Reading and subsequently used the Japanese woodcut method himself. Just a few years after Batten and Fletcher he started to produce a large number of bird and topographical prints. In 1927 Greenslade acquired seven prints directly from Allen Seaby, who was by then Professor of Art at Reading University. At the same time he also acquired two by Kathleen Hale, a student of Seaby who went on to gain international recognition for her *Orlando, the Marmalade Cat* series of books. Seaby developed the use of strong colour in his prints, sometimes printing the same blocks in different colour-ways. He often treated Western fauna and flora in a particularly Japanese manner. In the prints *Owl* and *Albatross*

Mabel Alington Royds (1874-1941) *Sunspots* woodcut 1913

he uses the *Ichimonji* technique - a band of colour which fades towards the bottom of the image - so common in many *Ukiyo-e* prints of the early 19th century. Seaby published an influential article on his techniques in *The Studio* in 1919 and later the book *Colour Printing with Linoleum and Wood* (Dryad Handicrafts, 1925).

Greenslade bought one colour woodcut (now missing) by John Edgar Platt (1886-1967) who was one of the foremost of the second generation of colour woodcut printers. Platt taught at Leicester School of Art and invited the Japanese artist Yoshijiro Urushibara (1888-1953), also known as Mokuchu, to demonstrate to his students. Six prints by Urushibara were bought from an exhibition of his work at the Abbey Gallery, Westminster in 1928 - his more intricate flower studies were four guineas each at a time when Greenslade was paying on average two guineas a piece. Of all the colour woodcuts in the collection these alone replicate the consummate technical skill of the *Ukiyo-e* printmakers of the late Edo period. Urushibara was born in Tokyo where he learned traditional woodcut printmaking. He lived in England and France between 1908 and 1934, exhibited over 40 prints at The Society of Graver Printers in Colour 1922-38 and exhibited in America after 1945. His own prints were executed in a variety of styles, but he is perhaps more widely known for his collaboration with artists such as Frank Brangwyn, George Clausen and James McBey, interpreting their designs and notebook sketches in the colour woodcut medium.

Allen W Seaby (1867-1953) *Owl* woodcut c.1925

Platt, in his own book *Colour Woodcuts: a Book of Reproductions and a Handbook of Method* (1939), noted the more abstract possibilities of the process, that it 'induces the use of typical form rather than accidental, and an abstract rather than a realistic attitude towards Nature'. This tendency is more apparent in the Japanese woodcut printmakers than their western counterparts, except for Platt himself and Ian Cheyne (1895-1955), but nonetheless Greenslade steered clear of the more modernist exponents of the genre. It is also significant that there are no examples in the collection of the Vorticist influenced linocuts of Claude Flight and the Grosvenor School. Morley Fletcher looked down on the modern linocut as facile, coarse and fit only for teaching school children. Flight, in his book *Lino-Cuts; A Handbook of Linoleum-Cut Colour Printing* (Bodley Head, 1927), retaliated with the pertinent accusation that the colour woodcut artists relied too heavily on technique and were 'lacking in any vital motives of expression in keeping with the age they are living in'.

Dorothy Lungley (dates unknown) *Fish* woodcut c.1930

John Platt was also vice-president of The Society of Graver Printers in Colour founded in 1909 one of the societies formed to further the cause of the colour print; others included The Colour Woodcut Society (1920), and The Society of Artist Printers (1921). In the inter-war years the market for colour woodcuts was far smaller than that for etchings but nonetheless were sold by several major dealers. The prints sold at an average price of one to three guineas and were a cheap alternative to watercolours in the middle class house or apartment. Sixty prints were purchased by Greenslade mostly from London galleries in the period 1922-1934; the majority were purchased from Colnaghi's (1931 & 34) and Harold Bromhead in Cork Street (1931-33). In 1923 he also bought nine woodcuts from students at London County Council Central School of Arts and Crafts.

Nine of the 22 colour woodcut printmakers represented in the collection are women: Jean Armitage, Mabel Alington Royds, Dorothy Lungley, Celia Ross Burnett, F Maude Klein, Kathleen Hale, E Dorothy Davies, Marjorie Abbott and Nora Wright. One of the foremost colour woodcut printmakers was Mabel Alington Royds (1874-1941), who exhibited in most of the specialist societies. She studied at the Royal Academy and the Slade Schools of Art. After teaching at Havergal College in Toronto she joined the staff of the Edinburgh College of Art where Frank Morley Fletcher was Principal (1908-23). Unable to afford pear or cherry wood, Royds worked on sixpenny bread-boards from Woolworth's from which *Sunspots* was printed circa 1913. She also produced many woodcuts of India where she travelled extensively with her husband the etcher Ernest Lumsden. Jean Armitage (exh. 1919-1962), a painter and printmaker who had trained under J D Batten, was probably the last of that generation of colour woodcut printmakers to practice the technique; she continued making prints for the Frost and Reed Gallery until 1962. After the Second World War the Japanese method of colour woodcut printmaking fell out of favour; artists tended to produce colour prints using oil based inks and used processes such as lithography and screenprinting which were more amenable to experimentation and the production of work on a larger scale. **NH**

Yoshijiro Urushibara (1888-1953) *Grasshopper* woodcut c.1927

Yoshijiro Urushibara (1888-1953) *Stonehenge* woodcut c.1927

Beatrix Holmes *Pray but one prayer* ink and silver leaf 1923

Margaret Bartels *Grant us the Will* from *a New Year Thought* by John Drinkwater ink 1923

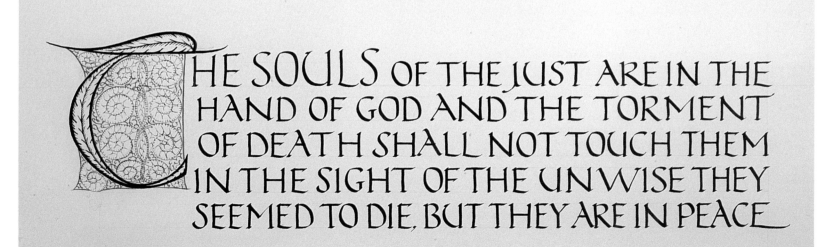

Lousie Powell (1882-1956) *Lidded cups with saucers* Wedgewood china c.1923-8

Calligraphy

The art of fine hand writing was central to the ideology of the Arts and Crafts legacy inherited from Morris and Lethaby. It has a long tradition in Britain from the monastery scriptoria of the Middle Ages to the master-calligrapher clerks of the seventeenth century who kept the accounts as English commerce expanded. Calligraphy was no less relevant in the early twentieth century. It was a useful craft readily applied to graphic design, commercial publishing and the private presses. Edward Johnston was the leading figure in the development of modern calligraphy. Johnston's sober, uncluttered calligraphy greatly influenced his pupils and his book *Writing and Illumination and Lettering* (1906) was seminal a text, generating an international revival of the art of lettering. From 1899 he taught calligraphy at the Central School of Arts and Crafts, an institution that encouraged excellence in design and craftwork.

Sidney Greenslade also was in no doubt of the importance of good lettering. In the *Annual Reports* (1925) he wrote, 'Writing is the most Universal of Arts. How few realise it is an art at all ... William Morris, Edward Johnston, and Graily Hewitt have been the great pioneers of the modern revival ...' The majority of the works he purchased came from the Brook Street Art Gallery, London, in 1923 after thirteen members of The Society of Scribes and Illuminators responded to Greenslade's invitation to 'execute examples of their craft' for the University. Subjects ranged from expressions of patriotism like *We Boys and Girls of the Principality* and Lincoln's *Gettysburg Address* to biblical extracts and similarly moral, uplifting passages: *Pray but one prayer* (William Morris), *Strengthen ye the weak hands* and *Grant us the will* (John Drinkwater). In 1925 he commissioned further examples from Margaret Bartells of the text, *Grant us the will to fashion*, 'to illustrate three methods of excellent modern "scribing"'.

All but two artists who responded to Greenslade's initial request were women, among them Beatrix Holmes, Miss L Puller and Edith Goodwin (b.1882). Women made a significant contribution to the Arts and Crafts Movement - not least as calligraphers. Victorian women had written and illuminated texts at their leisure, but the women's franchise and the opportunity of professional training in the crafts, gave women a tide on which to rise. Louise Powell (1882-1956), née Lessore, was the most famous member to respond, illuminating *The Souls of the Just* (1923). In her formative years she was in close contact with the hub of the Arts and Crafts Movement and was a friend of May Morris. She designed needlework and hangings, decorated furniture by Ernest Gimson of the Cotswold Group and worked with Graily Hewitt. She met her husband Alfred Powell at the Central School where she was a pupil of Johnston, alongside Eric Gill. She distinguished herself in manuscript illumination and transferred her skills to ceramic decoration, collaborating with her husband for Josiah Wedgwood & Sons Ltd.

Greenslade's stylistic preference was for uncluttered lettering and a harmony between form, function and decoration. These are rather formal inscriptions on vellum or parchment, which demonstrate the highly-prized skill of 'nobly spaced writing' and uniformity of letterforms. There are few stylistic differences amongst them though some can boast ornamental and gilded initial letters. Like many of the artists who practiced during the Arts and Crafts Movement, the calligraphers sought inspiration in the art of the Middle Ages and modelled their letterforms upon the simplicity of the Carolingian minuscule of the ninth century. **RM**

Louise Powell (1882-1956) *The Souls of the Just* ink 1923

Private Press Books

Blair Hughes-Stanton (1902-81) *Lamentations of Jeremiah* Gregynog Press 1933

William MacCance (1894-1970) *Fables of Aesope* Gregynog Press special binding 1932

The 20th-century private presses were also a legacy of the fin de siècle Arts and Crafts Movement. William Morris's interest in early book production led to the foundation the Kelmscott Press in 1891 to prove 'a work of utility might also be a work of art'. Ironically, the private press books were anything but utilitarian, they were expensive examples of 'self-conscious good taste' to be marvelled at rather than read. Kelmscott's elaborate and richly decorated books, however, were not typical of the books to follow. The best of the presses designed each book as a complete unit; the materials, type, page layout, illustrations and binding were individually designed according to the demands of the text (unlike Morris who enforced his gothic ideal on every book). The texts were usually chosen from the 'classics' assuring their popular appeal. The preferred medium for illustrations was wood engraving which could be printed letterpress in one operation alongside the type thus retaining the unity of the printed page.

Greenslade's first purchase with the income from the Davies Gift in December 1920 was eight Eragny Press books including Coleridge's *Christabel* (1904), Milton's *Areopagitica* (1904) and Keats' *La Belle Dame sans Merci* (1906). Eragny was set up in 1894 by Lucien Pissarro exclusively to print his own work and he undertook the entire production assisted by his wife Esther. The son of Impressionist painter Camille Pissarro, he introduced distinctive patterned covers and colour wood-engraving to the typically small format books with delicate illustrations and borders printed with matt water-based inks in pale greys, reds, greens and blues. Pissarro came to London with a letter of introduction to Charles Ricketts (1866-1931), founder of the influential Vale Press, whose elegant and inventive books epitomise the Aesthetic Movement of the 1890s. Ricketts did not own a press but he supervised every stage of the production at a commercial printers. *De Cupidinis et Psyches* (1901) purchased in 1921 is characteristic of the Vale's simple arrangement of type, generous margins and sparing use of illustrations. Ricketts' deliberately archaic black-line engravings are unashamedly eclectic, the illustrations show a synthesis of sources from Pre-Raphaelitism, French symbolism and Japanese prints to 16th-century Venetian books.

In 1921 Greenslade bought three books from the Doves Press established by Emery Walker, formerly Morris's advisor at Kelmscott. Without any ornament or illustration they rely solely on the clarity of type, its careful arrangement and simple page layout. A *Handlist* represents the work of C H St John Hornby 's Ashendene Press and *An Endeavour towards the Teaching of John Ruskin and William Morris* (1901) represents C R Ashbee's Essex House Press, a co-operative of the Guild of Handicrafts at Chipping Camden. There is one example of Sir Francis Meynell's Nonesuch Press which like the Vale was more a publishing house. Ricketts' finely tooled gilt binding, originally designed for Wilde's *The Sphinx* in 1893, was re-used by Nonesuch for Jean Paul Raynard's *Recollections of Oscar Wilde* (1932). *Passio Domini Nostri Jesu Christi* (1926), purchased in 1927, is not the most innovative or impressive of the nine books Eric Gill illustrated for Robert Gibbing's Golden Cockerel Press. A brilliant typographer and 'decorator' (his term) of books, Gill strikes a happy balance between primitive and modern. The simply defined black-line engravings drawn from mediaeval sources are in stark contrast to the technical virtuosity and modernist designs of Blair Hughes Stanton's engravings for the Gregynog Press.

Oddly, given the University's close association with the Davies sisters, Greenslade did not buy a Gregynog Press book until June 1927, four years after it began production. He then pledged to acquire a complete run of the books for the Museum, and as editions of some were sold out, the Controller Robert Ashwin Maynard took it upon himself to procure back copies. The Gregynog Press was the only successful venture to emerge from the sisters' intended arts and crafts centre for rural mid Wales. The press set out to publish Welsh works in translation, the best works in English by Welsh writers, and fine editions of texts in Welsh. Thomas Jones used his literary to find contacts for authors, editors and translators. The first book *The Poems of George Herbert* was published in 1923. Maynard and the press artist Horace Walter Bray left in 1930 setting up The Raven Press in Harrow only to close after four books; *Venus and Adonis*, *The Book of Tobit* and *Samson Agonistes* were bought directly from Maynard in May 1932.

Three of Britain's most technically brilliant and imaginative wood-engravers replaced the Maynard and Bray partnership at Gregynog in 1930. Blair Hughes Stanton, Gertrude Hermes and Agnes Miller Parker worked under the direction of the new Controller William McCance. Stanton's dramatic writhing figures in his finely engraved illustrations for *The Revelation of St John the Divine* (1932) and *The Lamentations of Jeremiah* (1934) were his *tours de force*, meticulous in detail and dynamic in concept. Likewise the subtle modulated tones and restrained stylisation of Agnes Miller Parker's engravings of flora, fauna and rural subjects for *Fables of Aesope* (1932) and *21 Welsh Gypsy Folk Tales* (1933) were unprecedented, whilst Gertrude Hermes' equally inventive illustrations for both Gilbert White's *The Natural History of Selbourne* or W H Davies's *The Lovers' Song Book* were not printed until the re-incarnated Gwasg Gregynog published the blocks in 1988 and 1992.

Loyd Haberly became Controller in 1934, but the Gregynog Press was never again to attain the inventive and innovative peak achieved by the unique partnerships which existed between 1930 and 1933; arguably they produced the best designed, illustrated and printed books of any of the private presses. The 'special' bindings from George Fisher's in-house bindery in particular have been internationally acclaimed. The social and economic climate, however, was the major contributory factor leading to the ultimate demise of the private presses, few survived the recession of the 'thirties and the original Gregynog Press too produced its last book in August 1940. **RM**

Women and Roses.

Lucien Pissarro (1863-1944) *Some Poems by Robert Browning* Eragny Press 1904

Eric Gill (1882-1940) *Passio Domini Nostri Jesu Christi* Golden Cockerel Press 1926

Ceramics

Studio Pottery

T he year in which Sidney Greenslade began to acquire ceramics for the Art and Crafts Gallery was a pivotal moment in the history of studio pottery. Bernard Leach and Shoji Hamada were in the process of establishing the St Ives Pottery in Cornwall; Reginald Wells had set up his kiln in the Kings Road, London in 1919 creating imitations of Sung-dynasty *chün* glazed pots; William Staite Murray began producing pots at his first kiln in Rotherhithe; Katharine Pleydell-Bouverie and Norah Braden were students at the Royal College of Art and the Central School of Arts and Crafts respectively; Charles and Nell Vyse in their studio in Cheyne Walk, Chelsea were experimenting with the re-creation of oriental glazes and Chinese high fired wares; and, in his summer holidays, Michael Cardew was learning to throw, decorate and fire pots under the tutelage of William Fishley Holland at Braunton Pottery in Devon.

The term 'studio pottery' is now used to indicate an enterprise in which the design and the manufacture of a pot is the work of a single maker whilst 'art pottery' is used to designate the products of a team of workers working to the brief of a designer. The majority of the studio potters in the collection were influenced by Chinese and Korean pottery of the Sung dynasty (AD960-1280). Large quantities of this ware had been discovered during the building of the rail network in China and were exhibited and collected in the West from the early years of the 20th century. Nearly four hundred pieces of studio pottery were purchased between 1921 and 1935, including the small-scale ceramic figures described later, forming what is now regarded as one of the foremost collections of pioneer studio pottery in Britain. Greenslade's selection of British studio ceramics was determined by the amount he could spend, his extensive knowledge of ceramics, his attitude to the crafts in general and the uses to which the collections were to be put - the instruction of students and trainee teachers in the methods and materials of good craft. He purchased the studio pottery at the new craft shops and galleries on his frequent visits to London, from the potters themselves and from various craft society exhibitions.

Greenslade's initial contact with studio pottery was his first meeting with the Martin Brothers potters in 1898. Robert Wallace Martin (1843-1923), Charles Martin (1846-1910), Walter Frazer Martin (1859-1912) and Edwin Bruce Martin (1860-1915) are often regarded as the earliest of the pioneer studio potters in Britain, although the dividing line between art and studio pottery is blurred in this instance. Robert Wallace was the main sculptor, Walter the thrower and Charles ran the shop in Holborn, London. The brothers' salt-glaze stoneware pots show a number of influences from Victorian Gothic Revival and French Art Nouveau to Japanese decoration. Greenslade was attracted to the work of Edwin Martin for its similarity to the work of contemporary French studio potters who were concerned with unifying body and glaze after the example of Sung dynasty pots. (It was not until 1925 that Greenslade acquired 12 pieces of the work of the French studio potters for the collection: Auguste Delaherche (1857-1940), Henri Simmen (1880-1963), Emile Decoeur (1876-1953), Ernest Chaplet (1835-1909) George Serré (1889-1956) and Martin St Honoré bought from the Georges Rouard Gallery at the Exposition Universelle in Paris.) Edwin's pots combined organic shapes, subtle glazes and an intrinsic 'truth to materials', a tenet of the Arts & Crafts ideology, which grew out of his knowledge of the process. A close friendship was established between the two men and over the next fifteen years Greenslade sent letters fortnightly containing ideas and sketches for new pots until Edwin's death in 1915.

Martin Brothers 'Wally Bird' and gourd-shaped pots, salt-glazed stoneware

Michael Cardew (1901-1983) 'Stork' slipware pie dish, earthenware

Bernard Leach (1897-1979) two raku fired drug pots & Shoji Hamada (1894-1978) celadon glazed lidded pot (middle), stoneware

Some of the pots Greenslade acquired appear to be by Edwin, but none of them were from Greenslade's own collection of Martinware, many of which are now at Pittshangar Manor, Ealing. Eight pieces were purchased in 1928 from the family of the late Dr Arthur Percy Allen of South Croydon and 16 from Arthur Punt Antiques, South London in 1935 for only £9-15-0. The rest were acquired from the Artificers' Guild (1922, 1935), A E Perry (1923) Bruford & Son (1926) and Heal & Son (1928). All the pots were produced between 1886 and 1907, including a 'Wally Bird' jar (1906) presented by the National Art Collections Fund in 1934, and all were fired at their kiln near the Grand Union Canal at Southall, Middlesex which they established in 1877.

Norah Braden (b.1901) left pair and Katharine Pleydell-Bouverie (1895-1985) right pair, ash-glazed stoneware

The attraction to Greenslade of the work of pioneer potters and their strenuous efforts to realise their ideas is exemplified in the 32 pieces he acquired by Frances Emma Richards (c.1869-1931), about whom very little is known. She had been working alone since the first decade of the century in various addresses in Highgate, London producing stoneware and earthenware pots in a kiln in her back garden. They present a great variety of forms and glazes, from monochrome to painted decoration and from vases to lidded vessels, but were considered ungainly and awkward by many commentators and contemporary collectors. He himself must have been aware of their shortcomings but perhaps the variety and occasional subtlety of form and glaze provided the students with examples of the rewards of single-minded determination. Richards' pots were purchased directly from her (1924, 1929), from the Mrs Summerday Gallery (1927, 1929), The British Empire Exhibition (1925) and from her solo exhibition at the Three Shields Gallery (1928). The following extract from Thomas Jones' journal of February 1933 is further evidence that Greenslade's personal taste was not the governing force in all his purchases. Jones reports to his wife a conversation with Greenslade: 'And the Hopkinses had a show. He [Alfred Hopkins] teaches pottery at Camberwell. I kept away as long as I could and felt such a coward for I new their stuff was bad. So I went in and they were sitting at the end of the room and nothing sold and I sat with them and the Secretary came in and out wondering if I was going to buy, but the things were appalling. They had tried to do birds - and they had no idea of a bird. I rushed out and bought nothing.'

However, Greenslade had bought over 36 of the Hopkins' pots between 1926 and 1928. Again the recognition of struggle and perseverance in the work seems to underpin the purchase. The Hopkins brothers had a pottery in Lambeth, London 1916-1932, then moved to Thanet opening the Stone Pottery. Starting as trade potters they became artist-potters and both taught at Camberwell School of Art. In the 1920s the Hopkins began working in stoneware and porcelain trying out various coloured lustrous and salt-glazes on often rather heavy oriental shapes, tiny vases and flute-rimmed dishes. Greenslade bought these directly from the brothers' pottery in Lower Kennington Lane, Lambeth at prices ranging from three shillings and sixpence to two guineas, but the majority at under £1. The invoices also advertise various services; firing, pottery supplies, moulds for slip-casting, restoration and private pottery lessons. Technical experimentation is the key theme in the acquisition of 50 pots by Charles (1882-1971) and Nell Vyse (1892-1967), including one of Greenslade's largest group purchases - 27 small vases and bowls fired in the Vyses' kiln in Chelsea, totaling £12-8-6 (1927). The remainder were purchased at P & D Colnaghi (1925) and Walker's Galleries, London (1928, 1930, 1932, 1924). They illustrate many of the Chinese glazes so influential in early studio pottery: celadon, *tenmoku*, *chün* and various ash glazes. Nell Vyse researched and devised the recipes with which the Vyses replicated oriental glaze effects. The results were often thought, by many critics and collectors, to be too similar to the originals to be worth acquiring.

Reginald Wells (1877-1951) 'Soon' ware, earthenware

The pots by Reginald Fairfax Wells (1877-1951) demonstrate his attempts to imitate the Sung dynasty *chün* glazes, and were made at his pottery in the King's Road Chelsea in the years after the First World War. He first made pots at the turn of the century at Coldham in Kent utilizing the methods and materials of indigenous medieval potters - some years before Bernard Leach was to follow the same path. The conjunction of the two influences and his struggle to master his chosen medium mark him out as *the* British pioneer studio potter. His 'Soon' ware, imitating *chün* glazes on oriental shapes predominates Greenslade's purchases, totaling 23 pieces, including shouldered vases, vases with small vestigial lugs, shallow bowls and a tripod-censer bowl. The pots were purchased, with accompanying carved wooden stands and bridges, from The Artificers' Guild (1922, 1923) and The Beaux Arts Gallery (1924). An article on Wells by Greenslade's friend Ernest Marsh (*Apollo* Vol.50, No.5 1925) makes particular reference to a small bowl in the Aberystwyth collection which is a 'successful combination of shaping and glazing and is an excellent specimen of its type'.

The effects of the limited budget and Greenslade's suspicion of affectation are manifest in the choice of pots purchased from William Staite Murray (1881-1962) which were the first pots Greenslade purchased, from the Artificers' Guild (1921, 1922). They were produced in Staite Murray's gas-fired kiln in Rotherhithe and again the goal was to emulate Sung dynasty pottery: they were priced from six shillings & ninepence for an ashtray to six pounds for a larger vase and bought with wooden stands. The highest price that Greenslade paid was 12 guineas for a 'globular pot' from William Paterson's Gallery in 1925, made in Staite Murray's new oil-fired kiln in Whickham Road, London in the year he joined the staff of the Royal College of Art. None of these pots exhibit the

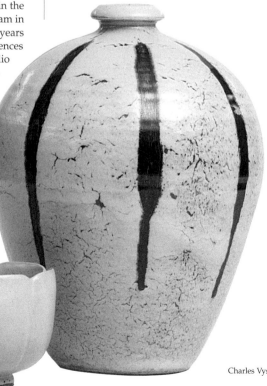

Charles Vyse (1882-1971), stoneware

William Staite Murray (1881-1962), stoneware

Stella R Crofts (1898-1964) *Barbary Sheep* and *Deer*, slip-cast earthenware

Wilfred Norton (b.1880) *Earthbound Man*, slip-cast earthenware

sculptural qualities or impressive dimensions of the much larger Staite Murray ceramics purchased by Rev. Eric Milner White in the same period, some of them priced over a 100 guineas; apart from the prohibitive price, they probably exceeded the boundaries of what Greenslade considered to be 'simple and unaffected'. The largest Staite Murray in the collection, at a mere 30cms in height, was a gift from the Contemporary Art Society in 1936.

The examples of Bernard Leach's work in the collection represent his early output from the St Ives pottery. They include five small raku fired pots, four inspired by the shape and tin glaze of Delft drug pots, purchased from an exhibition of the Red Rose Guild, Manchester in 1925. This type of pot Leach first made during his 'apprenticeship' in Japan c.1912; the cross-fertilization of western and eastern influences he likened to 'playing the seditious ape' (*A Potter's Work* 1967). The first Leach pot had been purchased from the Artificers' Guild along with eight Reginald Wells pots in 1922. Thereafter Leach's work was bought from the Beaux Arts Gallery (1933, 1934), The National Society of Painters, Sculptors, Engravers and Potters (1933) and the Three Shields Gallery (1933) at prices ranging from five shillings to £5. Most of the pots in the collection by Bernard Leach, with one or two exceptions, are not his most technically proficient work, but they do act as indicators of his progress as a potter in the early years.

Shoji Hamada (1892-1978), Bernard Leach's friend and partner at St Ives, also incorporated European techniques such as slip-trailed decoration on stoneware plates, bowls and jugs. Those produced at St Ives were purchased from one of his two exhibitions at the William Paterson Gallery in 1923, shortly before Hamada left Cornwall to tour Europe and return to Japan; three examples made at his pottery in Mashiko, Japan were bought at Yamanaka & Co., London in 1932. Many of his pots in the collection also employ oriental motifs, particularly the chrysanthemum, in combed and incised slip with a galena glaze on a large bowl and in blue-grey celadon glazes with cream inlay on a bowl and a lidded box. *Tenmoku, tessha, kaki* and tea dust glaze with wax resist are used on the other pots. Greenslade himself gave a wax-resist decorated bowl by Hamada to the V&A in 1924.

Greenslade purchased around 45 earthenware pots by Michael Cardew, nearly all them of produced at his Winchcombe Pottery between 1928 and 1933. A few are the work of Sidney Tustin who worked at the pottery from 1927. They were purchased from The New Handworkers Gallery (1928, 1929, 1930, 1931), the Three Shields Gallery (1933) and The Little Gallery (1933). Cardew alone of the early studio potters managed to produce a relatively affordable range of domestic wares - the most expensive piece here was two guineas and the cheapest two shillings. Cardew recalls in *A Pioneer Potter* (1969) having met Sidney Greenslade on a number of occasions, for the first time in 1923 at the headquarters of the Art Workers' Guild in the company of Wallace Martin: 'Sydney (sic) Greenslade and his friends were kind and encouraging, but stern. They took care to impress upon me that the society maintained very high standards of craftsmanship and that to be admitted to membership would be a privilege not easily to be achieved. But I did not perceive any compelling necessity to strive to achieve it.' The next time they met was in the summer of that year when Cardew arrived to work at Leach's pottery in St Ives. Greenslade is also mentioned in the context of his first one-man show at the New Handworkers Gallery, London in 1928 when, after a favourable review in *The Times*, Greenslade bought ten of the pots. Muriel Rose in *Artist Potters in England* (1955), describes the Cardew earthenware pots in Aberystwyth as forming one of the best collections of his early work and one 'which shows especially the rich variations resulting from his method of wood-firing'.

The work of Deborah Harding (op 1920s-30s), another potter about whom little is known but who featured in *The Studio* magazine several times, is also represented by seven pieces although according to the surviving receipts and invoices there must have been originally nearly 20 examples of her work. The first piece, a slip-decorated earthenware jar, was purchased in 1927 when she was a student at the Central School of Art. The stoneware pieces which are now in the collection have subtle poured and swirled glazes in white, creams, oxide red and purples and spiral motifs which emphasize the movement of the throwing.

Greenslade purchased the work of Katharine Pleydell-Bouverie (1895-1985) and Norah (DNK) Braden (b.1901) from exhibitions at P & D Colnaghi (1929, 1930), William Paterson (1930), Mrs Summerday (1931), The National Society of Painters, Sculptors, Engravers and Potters, Royal Institute Galleries (1931, 1933) and The Artificers Guild (1933). All the work in the collection was produced at Coleshill, Berkshire, the family estate of the Pleydell-Bouveries. After spending a year with Bernard Leach at St Ives in 1924, Katharine Pleydell-Bouverie set up a kiln at Coleshill and after three years was joined there by Norah Braden who had also been at St Ives between 1925 and 1928. At Coleshill the two potters collaborated in an investigation of wood-ash glazing techniques using trees and shrubs on the estate. Their work is often said to be indistinguishable and on some of the invoices the pots are described as being made by both women, but all Braden's pieces in the collection are clearly inscribed with her monogram. In an article in *Artwork* magazine (No.24, 1930) the critic W A Thorpe, referring to them as 'Bouverie-Braden' singles them out from Leach, Staite Murray and followers, as the studio potters who were most successfully creating an 'English' idiom from the example of their Sung-dynasty antecedents; by using low toned ash glazes the pots were 'a bit of landscape brought indoors and turned off into the round.' **NH**

Figures

The modelled, press-moulded and slip-cast figures, nearly seventy of which were acquired between 1922 and 1936, form a discrete group within the collection of art and studio pottery. The artists who made these small scale sculptures do not now appear in most of the histories of studio pottery - they were mainly, though not exclusively, made by women. The genre was popular in art schools from the first decade of the century to the mid 1930s when the market for this sort of ceramic figure suffered a sharp decline. Its popularity amongst female students is perhaps best seen against the background of the increased access to all manner of craft work as a leisure activity for women in the inter-war years. Although a hierarchy of crafts existed ascending from raffia, embroidery and weaving to pottery, there was a determined effort among the teachers and practitioners in Women's Institutes and art schools to raise the sights of their pupils above the various manifestations of the 'crinoline lady'.

Irene M Browne (op.1900-d.1943) *The Kiss* and Wilfred Norton (b.1880) *Into Whose Heart*, slip-cast earthenware

The first figures acquired were a group of six by Irene M Browne (op. 1900 - d.1943) purchased from the British Institute of Industrial Art in 1922. Their titles (*Hagar, The Kiss, Mother and Baby, Sisters, Grief*), subject matter and formal qualities epitomise the serious, even elegiac tone of many if the ceramic figures produced, during the inter-war years. They are finely modelled but not overly detailed and glazed in only one or two colours - subdued blue-greys, slate-purples, green and ivory. Browne exhibited small scale bronze sculptures from 1908, took classes in pottery-making at Putney School of Art in 1919 and thereafter began to produce a series of stoneware statuettes fired at the Fulham Pottery until she purchased her own electric kiln in 1927. Greenslade visited her studio in 1924 and she made a plaster portrait relief of him and one of his friend the collector Ernest Marsh.

David Evans (d.1959) limited edition slip-cast figures, Royal Lancastrian, Pilkington's Tile and Pottery Co.

The group of figures by Phoebe Stabler (op.1911-1955), purchased from the artist in the same year, represent the more decorative, colourful aspect of the genre. Their broadly modelled forms were obviously still in keeping with Greenslade's taste for 'simple and unaffected' work and although colourful, the glazes are quite freely applied to the forms. Stabler often collaborated with her husband Harold Stabler (1872-1945) on large scale, architectural work and on some of the larger figures such as *The Bull* - first produced in 1914 and press-moulded between 1922 and the early 1930s at Carter, Stabler and Adams Ltd, Poole where Harold was a director. Phoebe Stabler also sold her designs to Royal Doulton, Royal Worcester and Ashtead Potteries. Her smaller scale figures, depictions of women, children, and animals, conform to the dominant subject matter chosen by the ceramic modellers of the period. Greenslade seems to have acquired them in series to demonstrate the effects of variations in glaze and form (there are three subtly different versions of *The Lavender Woman* or *Madonna of the Square*, two in different colour schemes and one in an all-over golden brown glaze.) The figurative pieces in the collection were either purchased from her studio, Carter, Stabler and Adams Ltd. or from F & C Osler Ltd., and Heal & Son Ltd., London.

Stella Rebecca Crofts (1898-1964) became one of the best known of the animal figure makers. In 1927 Greenslade purchased four of her animal groups from her studio at Ilford, Essex; at prices ranging from three to six guineas each they were by no means cheap. On the invoice she describes herself as 'Studio Potter, Animal Modeller and Designer'. Crofts studied at the Central School from 1916-22, and subsequently at the Royal College of Art and after 1923 exhibited a number of bronze sculptures including contemporary and historical portrait busts. Her ceramic figure groups were praised by critics for their 'humorous' and 'virile' qualities (*The Studio*, 1924, p201) and censured for their concern with detail at the expense of basic form. Back-handed complements such as 'charming' and 'decorative' were often levelled at the work of many women modellers. The prime target was colourful figurative work with literary or historical themes invoking European rather than oriental antecedents. The work of very successful artists such as Gwendolen Parnell or for that matter the colourful slip-cast figures of Charles and Nell Vyse are notably absent from the Aberystwyth collection.

The approved 'oriental' concern with basic form is most apparent in Greenslade's purchase in 1923 from the Artificers' Guild, of five animal figures by the pioneer studio potter Reginald Wells (1877-1951) - two models of Indian Runner ducks, two rabbits and a cockerel. The ducks and rabbits are thickly glazed in variegated, muted colours with no emphasis on details of fur or feather. These were relatively cheap, ranging from 25 to 30 shillings each. The same relation between glaze and form can be seen in the *Owl* by Dora Billington (1890-1968), purchased from the artist in 1925 for three guineas. At the time Billington had just taken over the pottery classes at the Central School of Art. She also taught at the Royal College of Art and was renowned for her technical expertise among fellow potters and students. In 1927 Greenslade purchased ceramics and prints, from a group of six students at the Central School. Among them were two works by Sybil Finnemore (op. 1927-1961). Her modelled version of the Medici Boar and a small sgraffito decorated jar were illustrated in *The Studio* the following year in which the critic praised the tacitly masculine qualities of 'vigorous character ... and excellent craftsmanship' (Vol. 95, pp32-33)

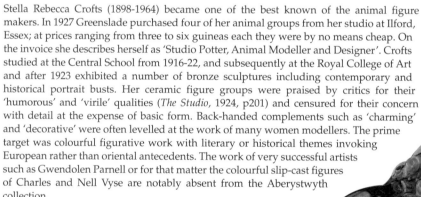

Harold and Pheobe Stabler *The Bull*, press-moulded stoneware designed 1914, manufactured at Poole Pottery, Dorset 1920-c.1930

Carter & Co., Poole, tin-glazed earthenware c.1910

Alfred H (1865-1960) and Lousie Powell (1882-1956) plate, vase and mug, lustre-decorated earthenware 1923-28

Between 1925 and 1926 Greenslade purchased eight ceramic figures from Wilfred and Lily Norton's Kerama Studio in Chalcot Gardens, London. These figures by Wilfred Norton (b.1880), small in scale but carrying weighty titles, included *Into Whose Heart*, *The World's Desire*, *The Becoming 'I am'*, *Earthbound Man*, and *Jeunesse* at prices ranging from one to four guineas. He must have been attracted to their simplified, almost modernist forms and sober, subtly modulated glazes. The aspiration to be considered seriously as sculpture could, of course, be realised by an increase in scale; Reginald Wells produced larger figures which were frequently regarded as trial pieces or maquettes for larger bronze sculptures. The only larger scale pieces in the collection are by Adrian Allinson (1890-1959): *Mother and Child*, *The Negress* and *A Peasant Madonna*. Allinson trained at the Slade and subsequently produced sculpture, paintings and prints; he exhibited work with the New English Art Club and the London Group. *Peasant Madonna* acquired from the Leicester Galleries in 1935 for 15 guineas was the most expensive single piece of ceramic purchased for the collection. At 41cms in height with an all-over white salt-glaze, its depiction of a particular female stereotype seems all the more exaggerated in comparison with others on the same theme. In view of the material and scale it may also have been an attempt by Greenslade to make a connection between contemporary ceramic figures and the busts produced by John Dwight's workshop at Fulham in the 17th century - Greenslade was quoted as an authority on the subject on more than one occasion (for instance by Ernest Marsh in an article on Wells, *Apollo* May 1925, p283).

In 1936 the very last ceramic figure to be acquired was a gift of the Contemporary Art Society of *Polly Peachum* by Agatha Walker (op.1911-1939), who produced a series of models of literary and historical figures. Representing as it does a character from John Gay's *Beggar's Opera* in 18th century dress, a 'crinoline lady', it forms a rather ironic codicil to the collection of ceramic figures. **NH**

Art Pottery

Greenslade did not buy ceramics solely from studio potters. He purchased a significant number of ceramics now categorised as art pottery; these were often produced in the existing centres of mass-produced pottery but were an attempt to exploit the growing market, at the end of the 19th-century, for non-utilitarian ceramics intended for domestic display. The larger pottery manufacturers employed craftspeople to design and decorate pottery allowing a degree of experimentation and an exchange of ideas which encouraged the dissemination of technical expertise, from throwing to glaze recipes to decorating techniques.

Greenslade's policy seems to have been to purchase from the range of contemporary practice, but conditioned by his criteria of 'simple and unaffected' work and within a limited budget. Examples were purchased from small workshops and the larger concerns which were part of industrial works. Included in the collection are examples of work produced by country potteries such as Upchurch Pottery, in Rainham, Kent, in operation between 1913 and 1963. From a bread-and-butter line of largely domestic and agricultural ceramics, brick and tile making, many country potteries were able to accommodate the demand for more decorative pots, and even compete with the Staffordshire and London factories in the market for hand-decorated wares at affordable prices. The Upchurch Pottery pieces were purchased by Greenslade from the Artificers' Guild in 1923. Greenslade may well have known about the pottery through his connections with Edward Spencer who wrote a pamphlet on the Upchurch Pottery (Women's Printing Society, London 1913) and was a founder of the Art Workers' Guild. They shared a mutual interest in the Martin Brothers pottery and were both friends of Edwin Martin. By 1923 the pottery was well established; it has been built in the first decade of the century by the brothers Seymour and Sidney Wakely. Seymour, possibly under the influence of his friend Reginald Wells, started to make art pottery in 1913, hiring Edward J Baker (1876-1955) a keen experimenter in glazes, who had previously worked for Wells and for Doulton & Co., Lambeth. There are three bulb bowls and a tall vase in the collection; their simple earthenware forms and subtly coloured, running, silky glazes, were probably designed by Baker himself influenced by Korean and Chinese Sung-dynasty pots and illustrations of ancient Greek and Roman pottery.

A slightly larger manufacturer producing both domestic and art pottery was J Bourne & Sons, Denby Pottery, Derby. In 1925 Greenslade acquired a 'Tideswell' vase, an 'Edenson' bowl and a 'Longstone' bowl from the British Empire Exhibition; they are glazed in various browns with very little surface decoration. The pottery was established in 1809 and acquired by Joseph Bourne in 1812, mainly producing domestic Denby Ware. In the same year these examples were purchased the firm had introduced Danesby Ware, a new line of pots decorated with tube-lining and much brighter greens and electric-blue glazes.

There is very little in the way of lustre-glazed pottery in the collection; an example of the work of William de Morgan was purchased c.1927 but this is now missing. There are only two items of lustre from the Royal Lancastrian wares produced by Pilkington's Tile and Pottery Co. Ltd, Manchester - a small lidded pill box decorated by Annie Burton, possibly given by J B Willans in 1915 and a green two-handled vase designed by F Lewis Day. The majority of Royal Lancastrian pottery in the collection consists of stoneware vases and bowls designed by Gladys Rogers (op. 1907-1938), William S Mycock (b. 1872, op. 1894-1938) and Richard Joyce (1873-1931), some of which were thrown by E T Radford (op.1903-1936). The Royal Lancastrian ceramics were mostly purchased from Pilkington's Tile and Pottery Co. Ltd (1930, 1935) and from the British Empire Exhibition (1930). The majority are 'Lapis' ware, a technique in which underglaze colours are covered with an eggshell glaze which softly diffuses the painted decoration. Gladys Rogers was largely responsible for developing the technique (invented by Joseph Burton). The elaborate decoration of some of the pots by Mycock and Joyce involved incising, carving and modelling the surface of the clay into low relief friezes of birds and fish before covering with eggshell glazes. The pots exhibit a range of influence similar to the earlier art pottery makers, from Japonisme to Art Nouveau and even Pueblo pottery. Despite the high degree of finish in all the Royal Lancastrian pottery in the collection the evidence of great hand-craft skill is always apparent.

Other than two Ruskinware vases given by the Welsh Arts Council in 1977 the only example of work purchased in the inter-war years that has any connection with William Howson Taylor's pottery is a bowl by E R Wilkes (1861-1953), labelled 'New Spectra' and purchased at the British Empire Exhibition in 1925. Wilkes worked for the art-pottery designer Bernard Moore in Stoke-on Trent until 1912, then with Richard Howson (brother of William) at the Ruskin pottery in Smethick, developing flambé glazes. Other purchases with iridescent or lustre glazes were few and far between. In 1920 Greenslade bought from the Burslem branch of Doulton and Co. four vases with a dark blue-green metallic glaze and faint iridescent decoration of plant forms (these are possibly from the 'Titanian' range designed by Charles J Noke, Art Director at Doulton at the time). In 1928 four pieces of Noke's 'Chang' ware were purchased, so called after Chang the Elder, a mythical potter of Sung-dynasty China. These four pieces are evidence of the importance of the chemist-potter's role in the art pottery industry; the glazes, unctuous, dripping, crackled and varicoloured on oriental shapes are the sole decoration. A large white Doulton jar, hand-thrown and indented in an oatmeal glaze was given by the Contemporary Art Society in 1936.

Greenslade acquired four pots from the Royal Copenhagen Porcelain Manufactory, Depot for the British Empire, Bond St in 1930 at prices ranging from £3-15-0 to six guineas. These include two pieces by Bode Bertel Willum Willumsen (b.1895) who worked for the company 1925-1930 and 1940-1948; an ovoid vase with lizard handles and a narrow-necked vase with three lugs; both are thrown, turned and glazed in brown overlaid with a grey-green running glaze. Willumsen designed stoneware sculpture as well as pottery and a piece of his work was also acquired by the collector Eric Milner-White in 1928. The 14 works purchased from Carter, Stabler & Adams, Poole, excluding Phoebe Stabler's modelled figures, are mostly early painted earthenware pots and experimental pieces by John Adams (including three stoneware bowls); there are very few of the highly decorated vases and bowls for which Carter, Stabler and Adams became so famous. Greenslade purchased the Poole wares directly from the company (1923,1935) and from the Mansard Gallery, Heal & Son (1925, 1927, 1928). One large painted vase was purchased from The Challenge Ltd, London (1933) for £2-10-0, hand painted in grey, brown and black by Eileen Prangell in a pattern designed by Truda Carter.

The collection of 37 hand-painted factory-made ceramics by Alfred (1865-1960) and Louise Powell, née Lessore (1882-1956) and their workshop of paintresses represents the continuation of a long tradition of European ceramic decoration. The Powells trained their work force on their thrice yearly visits to Etruria in Staffordshire. They produced their own work at their studio in Red Lion Square in London where it was also exhibited. The Powells were given overall control of the designs they produced for Wedgwood; much of it consisted of flora and fauna in keeping with so much Arts and Crafts Movement decoration, but which had precedents in Islamic ceramic decoration, William de Morgan's appropriation of these motifs, Louise Powell's own training in calligraphy and her study of the original 18th-century Wedgwood pattern books. The Alfred and Louise Powell ceramics were purchased from the artists (1924) or from the Brook St Gallery, London (1923, 1928, 1929). It is evident therefore, from the range of art pottery Greenslade purchased for the collection, that it too conforms to the general themes which underscore the rest of the inter-war ceramics collection - experimental but not flamboyant and looking to ancient traditions yet very much a part of contemporary practice. **NH**

Tall blue glazed vase, Royal Lancastrian

Richard Joyce (1873-1931) vase with fish decoration in relief, stoneware, Royal Lancastrian

William S Mycock (b. 1872) vase with carved fish motif, stoneware, Royal Lancastrian & Charles J Noke *Chang ware* pot, Doulton & Co., Burslem

Upchurch Pottery, Wakeham, Kent, earthenware c.1923

Glass

In 1925 Greenslade purchased four Lalique glass vases from the landmark *Exposition des Arts Décoratifs et Industriels Modernes* in Paris which launched the Art Deco style in Europe. This was not only to be the start of a collection of modern glass, but also one of French craft work, for he also bought twelve pieces of contemporary French ceramics. It was the only modern glass to be acquired by the Museum. However, the 'historical' glass collection began in 1923 developed very quickly, particularly since examples could be readily acquired. Both Greenslade and Dan Jones purchased the glass between May 1923 and January 1935 from antique dealers in Aberystwyth and as far afield as Exeter, Oxford and York.

There were no indigenous makers of fine glass in Britain until the 18th century, it was hitherto imported from the continent at a high cost. Wood, ceramic, horn or pewter drinking vessels were most commonly used until the chemist George Ravenscroft was commissioned by the Glass Sellers' Company to develop a clear English glass of quality. In 1675, using a high proportion of lead oxide, he invented a glass that was heavy and bright, and ideally suited to engraving. The Aberystwyth collection illustrates the subsequent development of glass making from a localised hand-craft to a large and profitable industry producing hand-made glass in Bristol, the Midlands and the North-East.

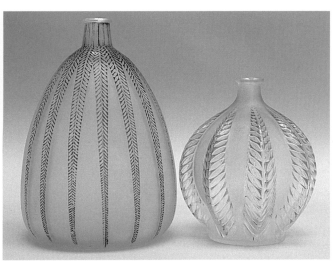

René Lalique (1860-1945) *Acacia* and *Malines* opaque glass 1922

The 18th and 19th-century drinking glasses demonstrate different means of manufacture and the evolution of form and decoration. The form determines vessels used for wine, liqueur, spirit, sweet cordial and ale. (A self-imposed social etiquette that emerged in the 18th century and persists to this day.) The earliest squat balusters with large bowls give way to the tall slender-stemmed vessels with small engraved bowls in the Rococo fashion and eventually revert to the more plain vessels of the Neo-classical period. The cut-off point appears to be the introduction of machine-made Victorian cut glass which was frowned upon by collectors and Arts and Crafts idealists alike. The air and opaque-twist stems represent the zenith of the glass-maker's craft, his skill evident in the complex construction and decoration. Opaque twist stems were introduced between 1755-1790 and the method of production was indebted to 17th-century Venetian *latticinio* ware. White enamelled glass rods were secured in cylindrical moulds into which molten clear glass was poured and then shaped to form multiple spiralling threads of varied thickness. The engraved flowers, vines, rose-buds and birds are typical of the period. One glass in particular has been made in the manner of a highly-prized early 18th-century Jacobite drinking glass, but the engraved rose probably does not correspond to the date of manufacture of the glass itself. The refinement of technical skills and increasingly sophisticated decoration in the late 18th century was paralleled in contemporary furniture-making, porcelain manufacture and silver-smithing.

18th & 19th century drinking glasses

The ethos of the native craft collection is embodied in the wine bottles *Neuadd, Carmarthenshire* and *Humphries Owen* purchased in 1931; they are of good quality, hand-made, cheap and of local production. The concern to illustrate the localised characteristics of glass-making, however, is best seen in the Bristol and Nailsea wares; spirit flasks, rolling pins, bottles, tumblers and a pipe. Bristol was a larger glass-making centre with 15 glass houses in the 18th century, more than London. The Nailsea Glass Works was established in 1788 by John Robert Lucas, the son of a Bristol glass bottle maker. Their glass-makers were trained under French and Venetian craftsmen. Only nine miles apart it was inevitable that there was a frequent interchange of ideas and personnel between Bristol and Nailsea. It is often difficult to distinguish between the two, Bristol glass tended towards brighter, stronger colours especially sapphire blue (sometimes with irregular flecked decoration in colours), whilst Nailsea glass is finer and more delicate in its decoration, specialising in the ribbon and drag-marbled flasks with transparent, white and multi-coloured glass decoration.

Greenslade paid 200 francs for the four vases designed by French goldsmith and glass-maker René Lalique (1860-1945) from the Paris Exposition organised by the government as a showpiece for contemporary French design and decorative arts. Lalique's small richly ornamented scent bottles with which he established his reputation had become synonymous with the organic Art Nouveau style, but by the early 1920s he had stream-lined his designs and diversified his range to include tableware and vases. Mass produced in Lalique's Paris factory, the mould-blown *Malines*, *Acacia* and *Tournai* frosted-glass vases with narrow-necked teardrop and ovoid forms typify his stylised, geometric leaf-form decorations of 1920-23.

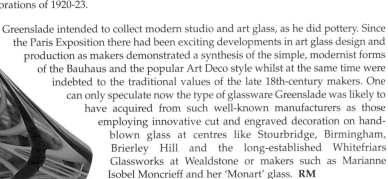

Nailsea Flask, early 19th century

Greenslade intended to collect modern studio and art glass, as he did pottery. Since the Paris Exposition there had been exciting developments in art glass design and production as makers demonstrated a synthesis of the simple, modernist forms of the Bauhaus and the popular Art Deco style whilst at the same time were indebted to the traditional values of the late 18th-century makers. One can only speculate now the type of glassware Greenslade was likely to have acquired from such well-known manufacturers as those employing innovative cut and engraved decoration on hand-blown glass at centres like Stourbridge, Birmingham, Brierley Hill and the long-established Whitefriars Glassworks at Wealdstone or makers such as Marianne Isobel Moncrieff and her 'Monart' glass. **RM**

World Craft

B y 1900 the Museum had amassed a substantial collection of ethnographic material from the gifts of individual benefactors. A Tasmanian boomerang, Peruvian pottery, a Hindu idol, an umbrella from Rangoon, paintings on mica, Siamese knives and a mushroom headed club ('taken from natives between Bombay and Pooma') are among the multifarious gifts recorded in the Calendar that year, forming a display of 'savage weapons and ornaments ... to illustrate man's work and life under the natural conditions of different regions'. (*Annual Reports*, 1901)

H J Fleure, who became Curator from c.1910, developed these collections further as an examination of human development in different environments and the use made of available materials. He devoted his life's studies to an examination of human evolution following a broadly Darwinian framework through the examination of the material culture of various peoples. Herbert John Fleure frs (1877-1969) was born on Guernsey and won a scholarship to study zoology at Aberystwyth in 1897 where, in 1904, he was offered an assistant lectureship in zoology, geology and botany. At that time zoology was the natural route through higher education for anyone interested in human geography which was nowhere recognised as a university subject. Fleure was a pioneer in the early history of Geography in Britain. He became the first Professor of Geography and Anthropology at Aberystwyth when the Davies sisters endowed the Gregynog Chair in Geography in 1918 (only the second Chair in Britain). He was Honorary Secretary of the Geographical Association from 1915 and Editor of its journal; numerous awards were bestowed upon him in Europe and America.

Fleure's theory that 'living things and their environment are inseparable and must be studied together' stemmed from his studies of Neolithic societies after the Ice Age. The innovations that necessarily occurred in agriculture to feed more stable and higher density populations he believed to be a turning point in human history. However, his comparison of contemporary foreign societies as being technologically equivalent to Western prehistoric societies, evident from the *Annual Reports* (1915) describing the new displays in the Museum, is now an outmoded hypothesis: 'illustrating the progress of Stone, Bronze and Early Iron ages with a special case for local specimens. Parallel with these are cases for Australian, American Indian and Melanesian-Polynesian exhibits as a "Stone-Age" work; also separate cases of Bantu and North African exhibits respectively, to illustrate a fairly simple grade of "Iron-Age" work.'

Kabyle oil lamp

Oriental ceramics from the 'historic and retrospective' collection purchased by Greenslade

Blanc de chine figures, porcelain, Chinese

Gilt buddhas, wood, Tibet

Bizenware figures, stoneware, Japanese

After his appointment as Consulting Curator, Sidney Greenslade assumed responsibility for purchasing ethnographic material, building upon the 19th-century collections of 'world craft' already in the Museum. From A Stear or H W Whittaker in Exeter and other antique shops in Aberystwyth, Cardiff and London he bought decorative and ceremonial clubs and paddles of the South Sea Islands, fishing spears and digging sticks, Kabyle ceramics, African musical instruments, wood and ivory utensils and head rests, Indian, Chinese and Japanese ceramics and bronzes, and native American baskets. In 1923 the Department of Geography and Anthropology and a large part of the ethnographic collection moved to 11 Marine Terrace. In the following year there was a major reorganisation of the Museum, when it was re-named the Gallery of Crafts, creating more space for the best specimens of ethnographic material. In the Gallery of Crafts the weapons and implements of the Pacific islands served to demonstrate 'human workmanship within the world'. For the Department of Geography and Anthropology they were invaluable teaching aids used to elucidate the instruction of traditional social structures, tribal ranking and tactical warfare, much of which was lost after the first European contact.

The impressive collection of weapons, mostly dating from the mid to late 19th century, illustrate different types of warfare: there are meticulously carved Fijian rootstock clubs, heavy throwing clubs, ironwood 'Gunstock' clubs and pineapple skull-crushers; a broad sharp-edged dance paddle from Tonga; serrated clubs from Samoa; Australian aboriginal boomerangs; a pair of New Guinea stone-head clubs from the Torre Straights Islands; a Maori staff club from Tahiti with pana shell inlaid eyes; a King Solomon Island axe with cut and polished pearl shell inlaid with designs of a frigate bird; and a finely chip-carved ceremonial Chief's Paddle from the Cook Islands decorated with the bold geometric patterning distinctive of the Polynesian islands. Their precise source and usage is somewhat vague, many 'exotic curios' such as these would have been picked up by whalers and passing travellers and they came with little documentation.

In the *Annual Reports* (1929) the Curators appealed to students and friends of the University for 'rare pieces of native craftsmanship brought here by missionaries and sailors from the south Seas and other distant parts of the world. Examples of these, such as paddles and clubs, food bowls and head rests, are also desired.' Musical instruments were also acquired to 'illustrate the life and art' of world civilisations, among them a *Sarinda* (an Indian fiddle), a New Guinea drum with a snakeskin tympanum (purchased from H W Whittaker, Exeter in November 1923), two African ivory war horns (from Mrs Webster, Gt Russell Street, London in November 1933), a south American violin with an armadillo shell forming the sound box, and in 1933 Professor J L André Barbier's gift of a group of African musical instruments including a south African *mbila* (xylophone) with gourd resonators.

From March 1924 Greenslade began purchasing small-scale cast bronzes and gilt Buddhas made in Tibet, India and Nepal; divinities of the type commonly used for domestic worship - *Nandi* (the bull of Shiva), *Ganeshi* (the elephant headed god, son of Shiva), *Ushnishavijaya* (a long-life deity),*Vishnu*, *Krishna* and *Vishnu Bhogasthanakamurti* - as well as a small number of Chinese wooden carvings and bronzes. In September 1925 he purchased from A Stear in Exeter selected items from the 'Garnham Collection' that Stear had acquired at auction. It comprised of a box of agates, stone implements and a range of Chinese, Japanese and Indian bronze figures and deities in porcelain, among them a casket, incense burner and impressive dragon-handled vase in bronze, and a good example of a Haida 'Pipe' (£1-15-0) - a totemic carving in argallite (slate) particular only to the Queen Charlotte Islands, British Columbia.

The 'historic and retrospective' collection of ceramics meant visitors to the Museum could profitably compare old and new craft - hence Greenslade acquired Michael Cardew and Welsh slipware, Leach, Hamada, Vyse, Wells and oriental pottery, contemporary figurative pottery and Staffordshire creamers, Pill pottery lions, *blanc de chine* and Bizenware figures. Bizenware (*Ko-Bizen*) originates from a small group of family potteries in or around the village of Imbe in the Bizen Province on the Inland Sea of Japan produced after the Kamakura period (1185-1337). Originally domestic vessels were produced with a high-fired red stoneware body, and during the period 1760-1880 giving way to statuettes of deities, animals and *koros* (incense burners) with a dark brown form of salt glaze. Greenslade purchased 18 examples of Bizenware between 1924 and 1926 from specialist dealers in Chinese and Japanese works of art - Ken Hoshino, Sicilian Avenue, Holborn and Shozo Kato, Oxford St, London. They include a gourd vase decorated with lacquer and pewter (c1830), two carp, an early 18th-century *Koro* of a sage on a tortoise, the god *Shishi* on a Peony, and figures of *Hotei*, *Fukurokuju* and others.

The *Tê Hua* manufacturers of the Fukien Province of south-east China were the main producers of *blanc de chine* ceramics for export to the West. The translucent ivory to chalk white porcelain with its unctuous and lustrous glaze was enormously popular here and significantly influenced European porcelain manufacturers during the 18th century. Production began from the late Ming dynasty (c1368-1644) but the 11 examples in the collection date from the 19th, possibly late-18th century: small statuettes of Buddhist deities such as *Kuan Yin*, animals, incense burners, and domestic vessels including the six *Libation Cups* purchased for £2 in August 1923. A Chinese celadon *koro* and a Song-dynasty vase are typical of the assorted oriental wares Greenslade also purchased for comparison with techniques adopted by the early studio potters. It comes as no surprise that Greenslade avoided the richly decorated Japanese Satsuma ware, it was far too ostentatious for his preference for 'simple and unaffected' craft, and besides it was already well represented in the George Powell Bequest.

The oldest known craft is also represented in the collection. Basketry reputedly pre-dates pottery and textile weaving - in fact the earliest decorated pots are said to have derived their designs from basket-work patterns. Basketry was enjoying a considerable revival in the 1920s. It was on the curriculum along with cane work in the Department of Art and Crafts at Aberystwyth. The collection was for the most part acquired in two groups. The first, in July 1923, comprised 18 modern baskets purchased for £15.14.6 from Dryad of Leicester. At Greenslade's request they were gathered together especially for the Museum by H H Peach, co-founder of the Dryad workshops, demonstrating different materials, methods of construction and decoration in basketry from northern Borneo (1), China (1), Germany (1), West Coast Africa (5), Ceylon (5) and from Peach's workshops (5).

Henry H Peach (1874-1936), an Arts and Crafts enthusiast and friend of W R Lethaby, was a founder member of the Design and Industries Association in 1915 (with Harold Stabler and others). It is possible he met Greenslade through Stabler. The Dryad firm was known for its fashionable utilitarian wicker and cane work furniture. Peach was a supporter of the National Federation of Women's Institutes, also founded in 1915. In its encouragement of traditional crafts and amateur handicrafts as a leisure activity, the Institute played an important role in the craft revival of the 1920s and 1930s. Peach set up Dryad Handicrafts in 1917 as suppliers of handicraft materials and tools, and the Dryad Press to produce technical booklets, to meet the ever-increasing demand of the women's institutes and craft departments of schools and colleges. The Peach collection was augmented in October 1925 by Mrs D C Davies, sister-in-law of Principal John Humphries Davies, who donated a valuable group of 22 native North American baskets from the Pacific North West and Alaska (*Haida* and *Tlingit* people), California (*Shoshone* and *Cherokee*), Arizona (*Chemuevi*), Idaho (*Nez Perce*), Washington (*Chehalis*), Oklahoma (*Pawnee*). Fleure's studies in regional consciousness also led to a series of publications on the anthropology of the Welsh people.
RM

Ironwood clubs, Polynesian, 19th century

New Guinea drum & African wooden artefacts

Native American (Cherokee)

North Borneo

West Coast Africa

centre: Queen Charlotte Islands (Haida)

Alaska (Tlingit)

Baskets

Lovespoon E Williams 19th century

Welsh Folk Craft

The interest in Welsh folk craft emerged from H J Fleure's broader scheme to demonstrate 'a sketch of human workmanship in periods and regions' around the world. Significantly, the collection developed at a time of growing awareness of the importance of local craft traditions in Wales. In 1927, some years after the University, the National Museum of Wales began its 'Welsh Byegones' collection under the direction of Iorwerth Peate who collaborated with Fleure on several publications on anthropology. As there were so few local craftsmen practising by the 1930s the curators worked quickly to acquire and document artefacts that were fast disappearing from the Welsh way of life. As the area of research developed its nomenclature changed from 'Byegones' to 'National Folk Art' reflecting the seriousness of their investigation of folk craft and industries. The collection formed at Aberystwyth, however, was more than a celebration of the material culture of country communities. It also stood for the 'dignity of craftsmanship', fitness to purpose and beauty of form integral to the ideology of the Arts and Crafts Movement. The ultimate attainment was the use of manual skills to provide for the needs of others in the community - the blacksmith, the shoemaker, the carpenter, the turner and the potter *et al*.

Dan Jones was responsible for the formation of the Welsh Folk Craft collection. He purchased from antique shops and sale rooms in Aberystwyth and around Wales, assisted by staff, friends and former students of the University who gave or procured exhibits for the Gallery. Appeals were also made to students to search their homes for unwanted 'byegones' to supplement the collection. The work of the blacksmith was represented by rush light holders, candlesticks, sugar and tobacco cutters, nut crackers, fire irons and dairy utensils; the wood turner by simple carved or turned domestic and dairy utensils - plates, bowls, rolling pins and ladles; and the woollen industry by a spinning wheel and weavers' fly pins. Whilst Lady Williams' gift of Swansea and Nantgarw china in 1915 illustrated that particular area of ceramic production in Wales, it was not deemed appropriate to develop this collection further for unlike native slipware it did not fall into the realm of folk craft.

The largest section of the Welsh Folk Craft collection was devoted to 110 pieces of slipware pottery - mostly baking dishes from Buckley in Flintshire, but also including examples from Ewenny in Glamorgan, and from Staffordshire, Devon, Lancashire and Northumberland in England. The curators searched in all parts of Wales for pottery to illustrate localised form and decoration as well as regional variation elsewhere in Britain. The first slipware was purchased in 1926 and was subsequently acquired by gift or bought for between 10 and 25 shillings a piece. In January 1932 Richard Pritchard of Anglesey sold 27 dishes from his private collection for which the curators paid a massive £110 in two instalments. In that year Col. Fossett Roberts of Aberystwyth gave two very fine Fremington (North Devon) harvest jugs that were originally made for owners in Aberystwyth *Ann Davies, Aberystwyth 1818* and *Ann Doughton 1827*. Slip is one of the oldest decorative mediums known to the potter. Slip-decorated earthenware has been produced by many cultures in most parts of the world, each country developing patterns and styles derived from their own culture and ethnic traditions. Dan Jones took a scholarly interest in this area of ceramic manufacture in Wales. He anticipated excavations taking place at the sites of old kilns and waste tips recording local forms and decoration, systematically identifying and documenting early wares and thus adding to the existing body of knowledge in the field.

Wassail Bowl Cover, Ewenny Pottery dated 1805, but probably later

Buckley slipware baking dishes, earthenware, 19th century

The long established family-run potteries at Buckley, like those at Ewenny and elsewhere in the north and south of Wales, were set up in areas where both clay and fuel were readily available. Buckley is principally represented by press-moulded oven dishes invariably decorated with a white or yellow slip - trailed, combed, marbled or personalised with inscriptions such as *Home His Home be it ever so Homely* and *Mary* purchased in 1931. There are also wheel-thrown domestic vessels such as storage jars, puzzle jugs, tankards and bread pans. Ewenny produced similar wares and also introduced a distinctive 'sgraffito' decoration in which the vessel was dipped in the yellow slip, which when leather-hard was incised to reveal the red body beneath. The low fired body was not very durable, the lead sulphide (galena) glaze flaked and eventually these wares could no longer compete with the finer ceramics and enamelled metal utensils available by the end of the 19th century. As a result of industrialisation, mass manufacture, economic competition and the improved transport of goods, country potteries and other small craft industries went into sharp decline.

Buckley slipware baking dish, earthenware

Simple items made for everyday domestic use, Dan Jones wrote were 'much more interesting and appealing than the work of the over-trained and often uninspired craftsmen of today' (*Annual Reports*, 1926). As such the collection of Welsh craft would, it was hoped, stimulate an arts and crafts renaissance in Wales - the Department of Art and Crafts purchased its first pottery kiln in 1927. The collection of early studio ceramics demonstrated that potters such as Bernard Leach and Michael Cardew intentionally imitated or developed the methods and materials employed by the makers of 18th and 19th-century domestic slipware. 'The craft of the potter is one that loudly calls for a revival', wrote the curators, 'Where suitable clay exists small kilns can easily be built without much cost, and so interest in a local pottery be fostered. It is a craft that readily lends itself to local expression. It can rapidly become "native". This collection should therefore be very helpful in spreading a knowledge and an interest, and so aid in fostering attempts at local revivals of this fascinating Art.' (*Annual Reports*, 1925)

In 1933 Greenslade visited J Kyrle Fletcher the well-known antiquarian dealer in Newport to secure his help in developing the Welsh Folk Craft, and in particular a love spoon collection. In a letter to Dan Jones, Fletcher wrote offering a range of artefacts from a shepherd's crook and bed warming pans to 26 love spoons, warning that because of the 'craft movement' items of folk art were becoming increasingly rare. (JKF to DJ, 31.x.1933) The giving of carved wooden spoons as love tokens during courtship and to commemorate special anniversaries is most widespread, though not exclusive to Wales. The spoons are the works of amateurs, not specialised wood turners, yet they are perceived to epitomise Welsh folk art. The Aberystwyth collection, acquired between 1926 and 1933, illustrated different forms and decoration evolving from simply carved spoons intended for domestic use to the increasingly sophisticated carving of the purely ornamental spoons. Few were documented - it is difficult to classify regional variation in love spoon making, or to date them with any accuracy, given that traditional patterns were copied over many generations. The symbolic geometrical motifs, subject to the idiosyncrasies of local craftsmen, also remain obscure.

Despite Dan Jones' special interest in vernacular furniture (for his Masters thesis he wrote on *The History of Welsh Domestic Art from the Sixteenth Century, as Exhibited in the Native Furniture*, 1925) the collection barely developed beyond a small number of country chairs, settles, oak coffers, tool chests and cupboards, probably due to restricted space in the Gallery. In 1925 Sarah Ellis of Narbeth presented the first major item of Welsh furniture - *a cwpwrdd tridarn* - an oak court cupboard which Dan Jones hoped would form 'the nucleus of a collection of 17th-century and early 18th-century furniture and household treasures' (*Annual Reports*, 1925). Only an oak coffer can be attributed with certainty to Sir John Williams' bequest, the other significant items of Welsh oak furniture are recorded as gifts in the *Annual Reports* - with the exception of a *cwpwrdd deuddarn*, an oak linen press purchased for £22 from I Balkin of Bangor in 1932. To collect simple utilitarian furniture of local manufacture seemed logical given the importance of furniture making within the Arts and Crafts Movement generally, and that furniture making was taught at the Art and Crafts Department in Aberystwyth; it was also introduced at Gregynog for a very short time. The more recent model was provided by the Guild of Handicrafts at Chipping Camden where Ernest Gimson and Peter Waals worked, the latter of whom designed furniture for Thomas Jones and the Davies sisters at Gregynog who were also patrons of Brynmawr Furniture Company in Gwent, established in the 1930s to produce simple Quaker furniture to Paul Matt's designs.

The collection surveying the history of rural crafts in Wales stressed the important contribution which native craftsmen and women have made not only to their communities but to Welsh culture in general. In their work both form and decoration were necessarily subservient to function, yet in these 'simple and unaffected' crafts beauty and function were seen to be at one. It was to 'such objects, more perhaps than any others', wrote Dan Jones, 'that we look for the inspiration of a proper spirit of craftsmanship.' (Morgan: 1928, p.198) **RM**

Cwpwrdd Tridarn, an oak court cupboard given by Sarah Ellis, Narbeth 1925

Wil Roberts (b.1910) *Hill Farm* oil 1981

Cedric Morris (1889-1982) *The Serpentine Pot* oil 1939

Thomas Rathmell (1912-1991) *The Sisters* oil 1953

Contemporary Art Society for Wales

There have been many public schemes to improve opportunities for artists working in Wales since the 1940s. Through touring exhibitions, competitions and prizes the Arts Council, the Royal National Eisteddfod and the Society for Education through Art all sought to promote Welsh artists and their work. One of the earliest endeavours to bring the best of Welsh art into the public arena was that of the Contemporary Art Society for Wales. Now in its sixtieth year, it continues to play an important role increasing public awareness of Welsh art and in helping young Welsh artists.

In July 1935 an exhibition of Contemporary Welsh Art was staged at the National Library of Wales and toured to the Glynn Vivian and the National Museum of Wales. The exhibition had been the initiative of a group of London-Welsh to bring art to 'the depressed areas of Wales'. They included Clough Williams-Ellis, Sir Elias Wynne Cemlyn-Jones, Augustus John and Cedric Morris. Encouraged by its success a second exhibition of 'Contemporary Welsh Art' was arranged by the Committee of Valiants and the Council for the Encouragement of Music and the Arts (CEMA) at the National Eisteddfod at Fishguard in 1936 to further dispel the myth that Wales was incapable of producing visual artists. The enthusiastic response prompted the organisers to put the exhibitions on a more permanent footing. Lord Howard de Walden of Chirk Castle, President of the Contemporary Art Society (founded in London in 1916), was invited to attend a meeting at Fishguard to discuss the feasibility of a Contemporary Art Society for Wales - to form a public art collection for public display. An executive committee of wealthy and well-connected individuals was formed - amongst them Geoffrey Crawshay, Viscount Tredegar and Gwendoline and Margaret Davies. At its inaugural meeting in London in April 1937 de Walden was elected Chairman and D Brynmor Anthony, an Aberystwyth graduate and Registrar of the University of Wales, appointed Secretary.

The Society was granted charitable status and funds were raised from the subscriptions of private individuals, companies, colleges and local authorities. Members were sought at a subscription rate of one guinea (an amount which remained fixed until 1976). One half of the purchase fund was to be used to buy art mainly by contemporary artists working in Wales, the other was used by the Committee to buy the work of established artists. Dr Thomas Jones was amongst the thirty-five members who had subscribed during the first year and it seems likely that as President he encouraged the University to subscribe as well. A purchaser, who was allowed complete freedom of choice, was elected each year and works of art presented to public bodies. James Bolivar Manson, Director of the Tate Gallery, made the first purchases in 1938, and the first distribution of forty-seven pictures to museums and colleges throughout Wales was made after the war, in 1946. Aberystwyth received an oil painting by Cedric Morris (1889-1982). *The Serpentine Pot* (1939) is typical of Morris's flower paintings in which he combined his two great passions in life - painting and gardening; the irises in the painting were hybrid species he developed himself.

In the next distribution in 1951 the University was presented with *Snowdon, the Treath and Frightened Horse* 1948, an outstanding early landscape by Kyffin Williams RA (b.1918). *The Sisters*, a large oil painting by Thomas Rathmell (1912-1991) followed soon afterwards. It is an important example of Rathmell's domestic interiors with figures and indicative of his commitment to figurative painting when so many artists at that time were exploring the possibilities of abstraction. Subsequently, about every four years or so the Society has staged exhibitions of recent purchases and invited institutions to submit a list in order of preference with the expectation of receiving two or three works in each round. At a time when Arthur Giardelli and David Tinker were expanding the scope of the University collections to include contemporary Welsh art and modern European prints (purchased with funds from the Calouste-Gulbenkian Foundation), no works from this rich source were presented to the University between 1961 and 1974, even though both Giardelli and Tinker were appointed selectors during that period. Tinker resigned from CASW's executive committee in 1975 when it was decided after pressure from the Welsh Arts Council not to include places of higher education in the distribution of pictures.

However, CASW donations to colleges were resumed and the works chosen by Tinker from those on offer reflect his commitment to non-figurative art. They included abstract paintings by Tom Cross (b.1931), Glyn Jones (b.1936), Eric Malthouse (b.1914) and a large canvas by Terry Setch (b.1936) *Thunderball (Axminster)* 1975. In the distribution of 1990 the collection of post-war art in Wales was enhanced by donations of paintings by Peter Prendergast (b.1946), Leslie Jones (b.1934) and *Welsh Hill Farm* 1981 an important oil painting by the Neath painter Will Roberts (b.1910) characteristic of his very distinctive type of expressionism. In the twenty works it has received thus far, the University's collection has been greatly enriched by donations from CASW. The breadth and variety of works reflect the objectives of the selectors, all of them professionals - art historians, museum curators, arts administrators, artists/teachers and businessmen. Works by established artists rub shoulders with those by the less well known. Some are traditional, some more progressive, figurative or abstract in a wide range of media, and of varied quality. The works reflect not only the tastes, ideologies and prejudices of CASW buyers but also those of the selectors on behalf of the institution. **RM**

the Great and the Good

Hubert von Herkomer (1849-1914) *Thomas Charles Edwards [Principal]* oil 1897

During a period that has witnessed the steady decline of official portraiture the University has maintained a tradition of acquiring and displaying portraits honouring not only those closely associated with the University's foundation and leadership, but also eminent Welsh statesmen, educationalists and clerics. The statuary was almost all acquired within the first fifty years of the University's existence - a time of enormous civic and national pride in Wales which saw the formation of the constituent colleges of the University of Wales, the National Museum and the National Library of Wales. These institutions demanded public sculpture and the growing national consciousness meant there was no shortage of patronage for Welsh artists. Most of the artists who won commissions were the London-Welsh; William Davies "Mynorydd", Joseph Edwards and William Goscombe John. These plaster casts, after marble or bronze originals, were invariably the gifts of subscribers or individual benefactors.

Goscombe John (1860-1952) was one of the country's most reputable sculptors of his day - his portraits, statuettes, war memorials and medals can be seen all over Wales. He sculpted the busts of *Sir Isambard Owen* (1901) and *Sir John Williams* (1903). In the Old College Quadrangle opposite the enormous statue of Lord Aberdare by Hubert Hampton (given by the artist) is Goscombe John's larger-than-life-size statue of *Thomas Edward Ellis MP* (1903), founder and first President of the Old Students' Association, whilst his bronze of *Principal Thomas Charles Edwards* stands on the seafront. Unveiled by Mrs Edward Davies in 1922, it was presented by subscribers following an appeal launched by John Williams to erect a memorial to the Aberystwyth's first Principal. Alongside is the only life-size statue of *Edward Prince of Wales, Chancellor of the University of Wales*. This bronze was commissioned at a cost of £8,000 from the Italian sculptor Mario Rutelli by his patron T D Jenkins of Aberystwyth. It was a gift in 1922.

The painted portrait of Principal Edwards by Sir Hubert von Herkomer (1849-1914) was presented by subscribers in 1897. A renowned portraitist, Herkomer was a Bavarian artist with strong Welsh ties and three-times married to Welsh women. Christopher Williams (1873-1934), the painter of allegorical and historical themes and portraits of many Welsh statesmen (including Lloyd George twice), painted the second Principal *Thomas Francis Roberts* in 1919. Numerous painted portraits were presented during these years: *Lord Aberdare* by Merthyr-artist W E Jones (given by Leyson Rhys 1877), *William Rees (Gwilym Hiriaethog)* 1877 by J D Mercier (given by the Deacons of the Independent Churches of North Wales), the poet and Wesleyan minister *John Williams of Caernarfon* by Evan Williams, *A C Humphreys Owen MP (Treasurer)* by G P Jacomb-Hood (given by his executors 1903) and *Stuart, 1st Baron Rendel of Hatchlands (President)* by Henry J Hudson (given by Lady Rendel). Sir John Lavery's oil sketch of UWA Governor *Miss E E Constance Jones* 1916 was painted at the end of her time as Mistress of Girton College, Cambridge where she had been a student of Moral Science. It was probably a study for the full-length portrait that hung at her home Lancayo House, Usk.

Tom Wood (b.1955) *Kenneth O Morgan FBA [Vice-Chancellor]* oil 1995

The inter-war years are very poorly represented but since the 1950s the University has started to commission its own portraits of Principals and Presidents at the end of their term in office. In 1951 Ernest Perry, Principal of St John's Wood School of Art, painted *Dr Thomas Jones (President)*. Henceforth, priority has been given to artists in or from Wales. These portraits are amongst the best examples of contemporary Welsh painting in the collection - *Sir David Hughes Parry, (President)* 1964 by Kyffin Williams, *Dr Thomas Parry (Principal)* 1969 by Alfred Janes, *Sir Ben Bowen Thomas (President)* 1970 by Ceri Richards and *Sir Goronwy Daniel (Principal)* 1978 by Thomas Rathmell. More than a mere likeness, the sitters have a personality and physical presence. Another outstanding painting which like this last group will stand the test of time is the recent portrait of *Professor Kenneth O Morgan FBA (Principal)* 1995 by National Portrait Gallery award-winning painter Tom Wood (b.1955) whose sitters have included HRH Charles, Prince of Wales and the playwright Alan Bennett.

Kyffin Williams (b.1918) *Sir David Hughes Parry [President]* oil 1964

The commissioned portrait presents a particular set of criteria to the artist, it has to pay homage to the sitter, fulfil the expectations of the institution and accommodate the sitters' pre-conceived ideas of how they wish to be represented for posterity. As art historical documents the collection presents an interesting survey of British portraiture over the past 125 years. **RM**

Ceri Richards (1903-71) *Sir Ben Bowen Thomas [President]* oil 1970

the Gulbenkian Collection

The poet, the conductor and the singer are part of Welsh life. But, not the painter - not yet. ... the hope is that ... when the students have become leaders and influential members of the society of tomorrow. In their homes, businesses, factories, and other places of work, and entertainment, they will find that the pictures and the piece of sculpture are needed.'

(Arthur Giardelli, undated leaflet for the collection, 1960s)

The loan collection of contemporary prints, drawings and small paintings was established for students to enjoy in their own private rooms. The scheme was the enterprise of the artist Arthur Giardelli, Lecturer in Art History in the Extra Mural Department. He aspired to interest students in original contemporary art and he persuaded the Calouste-Gulbenkian Foundation to help realise his vision with a one-off grant of £500. With this and an additional £250 from the Dr Thomas Jones Memorial Fund, Giardelli persuaded the University to contribute to the purchase fund from the General Account; £100 annually from 1963-67, and £150 from 1967-73.

The Gulbenkian Loan Scheme began in 1960. Giardelli shared the budget equally with Lambert Gapper until his retirement in 1962, then with his successor David Tinker. All three were committed to the notion of art for public places and in the belief that students' lives were enriched by living with works of art. With this conviction David Tinker resigned from the executive committee of CASW in 1975 after it had passed a motion not to continue donating art works to colleges in Wales. 'Who goes into art galleries but the converted?', he wrote, 'Maybe there will be even less converts if you cut out the centres of higher education'. (Letter DT to CASW, 24.iii.1975)

Initially the scheme allowed for pictures to be chosen from the collection by the wardens and sub-wardens of halls. In 1968 a new system of distribution was introduced. An exhibition in the Old College gallery, 'A Picture for your Room in Hall', was staged in the first weeks of each Michaelmas term and students were invited to make their own choice and hire a picture for a year; firstly at 2/6 (12p) and later 5/- (25p). The rationale which underpinned the nature of the works they acquired was explained by Arthur Giardelli, 'I had in mind to bring to Wales what original works I could get from the continent (mainly prints of course) so as to show what was done elsewhere than London which had dominated Wales all too long: hence Matisse, Picasso, Leger and the lesser and lesser lights. At the same time I wanted to show Welsh artists like Kyffin, Ceri and David Jones in relation to Europe rather than England - in Ceri's case, and David's also, so much more relevant.' (Letter Giardelli to Alistair Crawford, 3.v.1978)

Stanley William Hayter (1901-88) *Combat* engraving and etching 1953

Joseph Herman (b.1911) *Two Miners* lithograph 1950s

Pablo Picasso (1881-1973) *Colombe* lithograph 1952

Raoul Dufy (1877-1953) *La Danse* woodcut c.1910

Around 140 works were eventually purchased of which 46% were bought in Wales, 24% in Paris and 30% in London, representing not only the work of British and French artists but also Polish, German, Russian, Italian, Dutch, Australian, and Japanese. The works were all on a relatively small scale appropriate for the size of students' rooms in hall. Galleries and artists sympathetic to the educational aims of the scheme almost always gave generous discounts. Gapper's first purchases in 1960 included oil paintings by Gwilym Pritchard and John Baum, drawings by Mildred Eldridge and large colour relief prints by James T A Osborne (his brother-in-law). When the cost of an average purchase was £10 (£25 by 1970) the buyers were compelled to be resourceful. David Tinker called upon artists who had been given exhibitions in the Old College gallery in addition to his friends and members of the 56 Group Wales - Robert Hunter, John Wright and Eric Malthouse. Giardelli, who was a frequent visitor to the continent, indulged his passion for the School of Paris artists buying prints by Braque, Chagall, Dufy, Leger, Picasso and Pignon - albeit in cheaper unsigned and unlimited editions.

There are 114 prints in all representing the work of 75 artists. As well as the artists listed above the Gulbenkian Collection includes works by Edward Bawden, Stanley Hayter, Henry Moore, Sidney Nolan, John Piper, William Scott and Graham Sutherland. The scheme also served to encourage Welsh artists and artists working in Wales, the up and coming among those already established - George Chapman, Joseph Herman, Eric Malthouse, John Petts, Ceri Richards, Will Roberts and Kyffin Williams. Several important examples of contemporary Welsh painting were purchased with separate funds, most notably *A Cardiganshire Farm* by John Elwyn (b.1916) from an exhibition at the National Library of Wales in 1959 and in the following year there was a major coup for Giardelli when he acquired *Tulips*, an oil painting by Ceri Richards (1903-1971) from the artist's retrospective exhibition at the Whitechapel Gallery in London. In 1954 the National Museum of Wales had presented four oil paintings from the estate of the Swansea painter Evan Walters (1893-1951).

Fernand Léger (1881-1955) *Tete Bleue* screenprint 1952

There have been numerous public schemes and School's Loan Collection formed in the spirit of the Gulbenkian Loan Scheme and run by provincial museums and Local Education Authorities - but few have compared with the internal loan scheme at Aberystwyth. Alas, all have been dogged by similar problems leading to their eventual demise: the heavy burden of administration, the safeguarding of works against damage and theft, maintaining environmental control, and especially a lack of financial and human resources. In 1974 Giardelli wrote to the Registrar asking for more money - without success; he considered £150 was no longer sufficient to maintain standards. Collecting ceased and by 1976 the student interest in the scheme was at an all time low, only five of the 140 pictures on offer were requested for loan by students. For the first time that year the scheme was extended to include academic and administrative staff, common rooms and other public areas in the University.

Over the years the value of many of the items have risen significantly and works were withdrawn to join the print collection where they could be safely stored and looked after in the correct environmental conditions. The majority of these now form part of the Collection of Graphic Art and a proportion of them is still on loan to staff throughout the University. Whilst it was never the intention that the Gulbenkian Collection should be seen in the context of the existing print collection, it has nonetheless greatly enhanced and widened the scope of the Collection overall. **RM**

Ernest Zobole (b.1927) *The Valley* gouache 1962

Robert Colquhoun (1914-1962) *Trinket Seller* lithograph 1948

Dave Daggers (b.1956) *Stomboli* photograph 1987

Geoffrey Fuller (b.1936) earthenware figurative group 1990

the Catherine Lewis Trust

In 1962 David Tinker succeeded Lambert Gapper as Curator of the Museum, and in the following summer vacation he arranged for an inventory to be made of ceramics, prints and paintings. He then organised displays of glass, Welsh pottery and woodwork around the University, believing the collection too heterogeneous to display *in toto*. In October 1962 he prepared a report suggesting rationalising the collection in order to consolidate and extend the visual arts. Minor artefacts he proposed to loan to other museums or sell to provide funds to build up the strongest areas. His policy to 'sell to reinforce' was approved by the University but not instigated for some time. Thereafter he concentrated principally on arranging exhibitions of contemporary art.

During the 1950s travelling exhibitions of contemporary art organised by the Welsh Arts Council had been held in the 'College Quadrangle Gallery' which was inaugurated in 1948. David Tinker campaigned for a more appropriate exhibition space to attract more prestigious exhibitions to Aberystwyth. The new art gallery, in a large room over-looking the sea, was opened by the Lady Ruth Eldrydd Davies of Plas Dinam in November 1963. The development of the Penglais campus that had began in the 1930s and gained considerable momentum by the 1960s, culminated in the opening of the Great Hall complex in 1970 (later Aberystwyth Arts Centre). David Tinker was closely involved in the planning of the gallery there which was to succeed the gallery in town.

Tinker also campaigned for the teaching of art to gain autonomy from the Department of Education and in 1973 the 'Visual Art Department' was created and housed in the refurbished Department of Dairy Bacteriology on Llanbadarn Road. Two newly appointed staff members, Moira Vincentelli as Tutor in Art History in 1971 and Alistair Crawford as Lecturer in Graphic Art in 1974, took a special interest in the now languishing art and crafts collections and once more their importance as a teaching and research resource was appreciated. The task of gathering together, cataloguing and caring for the collection was voluntarily undertaken by Crawford who assumed responsibility for the prints and drawings and Vincentelli who documented paintings, ceramics and objets d'art.

In 1974, with no source of funding, or the likelihood of money being made available for the preservation and display of the collections, it was reluctantly agreed to sell a group of netsukes from the former General Museum. The proposed sale of weapons and ethnographic material planned for 1976 was thwarted at Senate, however, and as a result Principal Goronwy Daniel set up a Finance and General Purposes Committee working party in September 1975 to review the collections, chaired by Professor van Velsen of the Sociology Department. The committee acknowledged the huge contribution already made by Crawford and Vincentelli and formally recognised them as Honorary Keepers. The committee administered the 'College Art Collection Fund' comprising interest from the recently 'unearthed' residue of the Davies Gift of 1918 (then about £150 annually) and the proceeds from the netsuke sale. In May 1978 F&GP recommended that a joint Senate-Council 'College Collections' committee be established: 'to supervise the custody and display of artistic, museum and other objects ... and contribute to the cultural life of the College'. (*Terms of Reference*, December 1978) With a small regular income, and financial handouts from the University's general account, a programme of cataloguing, mounting and restoration began - progress was piecemeal and slow.

At a time of severe cut-backs in British universities, and when sources for funds for the collections had all but dried up, the Elvet Lewis Bequest brought a long-awaited reversal of fortunes. In 1981 Lewis died leaving his estate to the University in memory of his wife 'for the purchasing for the College works of art'. Dr Elvet Lewis was born in Aberfan in 1904, he studied Chemistry at Aberystwyth 1923-26, and was until his retirement Headmaster of Ilford Grammar School in Essex where he lived with his wife Catherine (1905-53). It was felt that since the existing collection was in need of care and in some cases urgent conservation, the spirit of the bequest should also be taken to include preservation and display - to make the collection accessible to as wide an audience as possible. The Catherine Lewis Trust Fund which is administered by the Committee, has provided two purpose-built galleries to house the collections: the Catherine Lewis Gallery and Print Room in the Hugh Owen Library opened in 1984 and the Ceramic Gallery in 1986. An active programme of acquisitions resumed to build upon the existing collections of graphic art and studio ceramics. With proper facilities for storage and display, in a safe and environmentally controlled conditions, the University was eligible for public funding towards the collections management and purchase of work of art - from the Council for Museums in Wales and the Museum and Galleries Commission / Victoria & Albert Museum Purchase Fund and the National Art Collections Fund respectively.

When government policy changed in the early 1990s to make museum funding more selective the structure was already in place to allow for the smooth transition to professional status as a Registered Museum in 1992, allowing public funding to continue. The move of the School of Art to the Edward Davies Chemical Laboratories in December 1993 created further possibilities for activities related to the collections, and most recently a successful Heritage Lottery application has provided a Print Reference Room to re-house the collection of Graphic Art in the Edward Davies Building in 1997. **RM**

The print collection had suffered years of neglect by the time Alistair Crawford came to Aberystwyth in January 1974. Many of Greenslade's acquisitions for the Gallery of Crafts had been sent out to halls of residence and staff common rooms before the Second World War or relegated to various store cupboards, where they remained unloved and unwanted. In the following years Crawford gathered them together to create an inventory and according to the inter-war records that have survived, the collection was by no means complete. However, it was once more looked after (albeit with no financial or additional human resources) and used for teaching. In 1975 a student print collection was established to which new acquisitions have been added from annual degree exhibitions. With the promise of a small display/storage area in the Hugh Owen Library, Crawford applied to a number of grant-aiding institutions to re-establish a purchase fund. Between 1978 and 1981 small annual grants from the West Wales Arts Association were matched by the University (totalling £300) to allow the modest acquisition of prints to resume. The aim was to bring the collection up to date and representative of the work of contemporary Welsh, British and international artists.

In line with the budget the purchases were modest - just three prints in the first year, by David Hockney (b.1937), Joseph Herman (b.1911) and Zoran Music (b.1909) purchased directly from the artist in Paris by Arthur Giardelli who was invited to spend a half of the grant that year. In the years that followed Crawford, to maximise his allocated budget, negotiated favourable reductions with galleries, dealers and artists with whom he had built up a professional relationship as a practicing artist. Up to 40% discount, for example, was obtained from the Curwen Gallery, London whilst other sources included Marlborough Fine Art and Editions Alecto in London, the Andrew Knight Gallery in Cardiff, and peripatetic picture dealers such as Anthony Dawson and Jonathan Phipps among the many agents in the 1970s selling to colleges, hospitals, local authorities and industry. Between 1978 and 1984 when the first income from the Catherine Lewis Trust was used for acquisitions, the University acquired by purchase and donation 113 prints representing 58 artists, including prints by Norman Ackroyd (b.1938), Edward Bawden (1903-89), Chloe Cheese (b.1952), Mary Fedden (b.1915), Terry Frost (b.1915), David Gentleman (b.1930), Anthony Gross (1905-84), Glynn Boyd Harte (b.1948), Gertrude Hermes (1901-83), Paul Nash (1889-1946), Victor Pasmore (b.1908), Ceri Richards (1903-71), Michael Rothenstein (1908-93), Bartolomeo dos Santos (b.1931), Valerie Thornton (1931-91) and Julian Trevelyan (1910-88).

The Elvet Lewis Bequest in 1981 helped realise the ambition to have a purpose built print room and gallery to store and display the University's extensive collection of works of art on paper - not only Greenslade's purchases, the valuable items withdrawn from the Gulbenkian loan scheme, and the recent acquisitions, but drawings, watercolours and nearly 300 prints by European artists from the 15th to the end of the 19th century from the George Powell and John Williams bequests (see AC:1984 pp.31-3). In 1984, the Welsh Arts Council funded the publication of a catalogue of the print collection by Alistair Crawford to coincide with the opening of the Catherine Lewis Gallery by vice-president Benjamin G Jones. During the planning and construction of the Gallery no interest was used from the Catherine Lewis Trust for acquisitions until the 1984-5 session. The aim has since been to acquire prints and drawings by contemporary British artists, particularly groups of works that are retrospective surveys of individual artist's careers; works by artists practicing during the period since Greenslade ceased collecting in 1935, with a view to consolidating the 1921-1935 collection with prints not already represented; important European prints, as funds allow, and to 'fill gaps within the existing collection by purchase of acclaimed printmakers so that it may be representative of the highest achievements of the history of printmaking'. The Acquisitions Policy pays respect to the collection's needs as a whole 'to acquire prints that are useful in the teaching and understanding of the history of printmaking, particularly with regard to the history of process'. (*Acquisitions Policy*)

Francisco Jose Goya (1747-1828) *Nohubo Remedia*, from *Los Caprichos* etching and aquatint c.1793-8

Terry Willson (b.1948) *Anonymous Portrait - Paris* etching and aquatint 1979

Bernard Cheese (b.1925) *The Drum Major* lithograph 1953

Victor Pasmore (b.1908) *Square Motif* etching and aquatint 1975

Glyn Boyd Harte (b.1948) *Cocktails* lithograph 1984

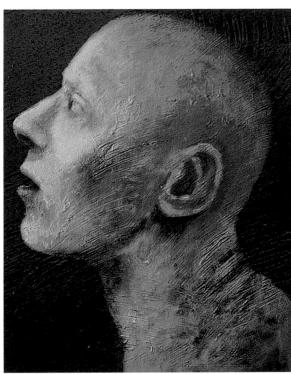

John Kirby (b.1949) *Head* screenprint and woodblock 1990

Little documentation has survived to determine with any certainty the provenance of the pre-1900 European prints in the collection, they are likely to be from the combined bequests of Powell of Nanteos and Sir John Williams together with numerous individual gifts to the General Museum, such as the 'portfolio of old engravings' recorded in the University *Calendar* (1900). Until they ceased trading in February 1988, Craddock and Barnard, London was the principal source of European prints to make good the notable omissions in the collection: among them Pierre Bonnard (1867-1947), Jaques Callot (1592-1635), John Sell Cotman (1782-1842), John Crome (1769-1921), Honore Daumier (1808-79), Francisco Goya (1747-1828), Wenceslaus Hollar (1607-77), William Nicholson (1872-1949) and Anthony van Dyck (1599-1641). Since 1990 Abbott and Holder, a few doors away from Craddock and Barnard in Museum Street, have helped to consolidate the University's holdings of prints from the inter-war years: works aquired by Stanley Anderson (1884-1966), Douglas Percy Bliss (1900-84), Edward Bouverie Hoyton (1900-88), Frank Brangwyn (1867-1956), Paul Drury, Herbert Andrew Freeth (1912-1987), F L Griggs, Laura Knight (1877-1970), James McBey (1883-1959), Mortimer Menpes (1885-1938), Orovida Pissarro (1893-1960), Frederick Richards, Louis Rosenburg (1890-), William Strang (1859-1921) and Leon Underwood (1890-1975).

The collapse of the print market in the 1930s was followed by the war during which time materials for printmaking were scarce and few opportunities existed for artists to make prints. In the meantime Continental modernism was making its presence felt in Britain and artists were gradually coming around to the School of Paris artists such as Pablo Picasso, Henri Matisse and Georges Braque (whose prints Giardelli was to purchase for the Gulbenkian Collection). After the war printmakers found themselves in a state of artistic conflict - the small black and white etching that had once been popular had now come to represent all that was moribund and old fashioned with its emphasis on skill and `tradition'. Many artists, sharing the optimism in Britain in the years leading up to and following the Festival of Britain in 1951, seized the opportunity for a fresh challenge and reflected in their work the change in attitudes that had occurred.

Post-war printmakers commonly took up media other than etching which was too tied up with the establishment and traditional values. Lithography was the preferred medium of the young generation of painter-printmakers, many of whom had worked for Shell-Mex, BP and London Underground between the wars producing large lithographic posters for the commercial presses. Poster prints became popular; original lithographs that were mass produced for schools, cafes and public houses. The first had been Contemporary Lithographs Ltd., begun by Robert Wellington of the Zwemmer Gallery and John Piper whose *Abstract Composition* (1937) from the series is in the Gulbenkian Collection. The Schools Prints series (1946) similarly encouraged painters to make prints in large editions to be sold cheaply - Julian Trevelyan's *Harbour* (1947) and Hans Tisdall's *Fisherman's Hut* (1947) from this series were purchased in 1989. The Miller's Press in Lewes, Sussex set up in 1945 by two sisters of independent means, Caroline Lucas and Frances Byng-Stamper, also helped establish lithography as a fine art medium by encouraging painter-printmakers. Miller's collaborated the Redfern Gallery in Cork Street who provided one of the few outlets for modern prints staging exhibitions by 'The Society of London Painter-Printers' whose show in 1948 included two lithographs *Yellow Still Life* by Robert MacBryde (1913-66) and *Trinket Seller* by Robert Colquohoun (1914-1962) purchased from Goldmark Gallery, Uppingham in 1993. As the artists' scale of values became international there was drift away from the sombre colouration of the war-time Neo-romantics towards abstraction and a positive use of bold colour. In 1951 Schools Prints Ltd. and the Artists International Association published the Festival of Britain series and in a signed limited edition devoted to aspects of contemporary British life. This suite is represented in the collection by Keith Vaughan's *Festival Dancers* and Edwin la Dell's *MCC at Lords*. By the 1950s lithography was being taught in art schools. In 1953 Edwin la Dell (1917-70) organised and published the Coronation Suite at the Royal College of Art where he had succeeded Robert Austin as Professor of Engraving, this portfolio of 40 lithographs is represented in the collection by his own *Band in the City* and *The Drum Major* by Bernard Cheese (b.1925), both purchased in 1993.

The only significant publisher in the 1950s to create opportunities for artists to make and exhibit intaglio prints was the Hon. Robert Erskine who set up St George's Gallery Prints in Cork Street in 1954, which ran until 1963 when he sold out to Editions Alecto. He encouraged painters 'who showed strong graphic potential' to produce large scale etchings in suites, revitalising the medium and generating a renewed interest for the medium amongst the public. Vertical Suit in Black by Merlyn Evan (1910-73) was published in 1958, from which derives *Helmet Head* purchased in 1993, and in 1960 the Rhondda Suite by George Chapman (1908-93) all six prints of which were purchased in 1987. By the 1960s there was a boom in the print market encouraged by the Redfern Gallery, the Curwen Gallery and numerous other publishers and galleries who supported a growing interest in prints, which was to continue well into the 1970s. David Hockney, who has consistently demonstrated an affinity for printmaking, emerged as the most versatile of his generation of printmakers, working in a wide range of media and subject matter. Significantly his *One Night* from the Cavafy Set (1966), bought from Editions Alecto, was the first acquisition when collecting resumed in 1979. In recent years attention has shifted towards the acquisition of artists' collections of their own work, but nonetheless important examples of contemporary British printmaking has been purchased, mainly from the Flowers East Gallery: Peter Howson (b.1958), John Kirby (b.1949), Jock MacFadyen (b.1950) among them. In 1994, two of Wales' most distinguished artists, generously donated prints to the collection, John Elwyn (b.1916) gave ten lithographs and Kyffin Williams RA (b.1918) presented ten of his linocuts on the occasion of the opening of the School of Art in 1994. **RM**

contemporary collecting: Artists' Collections

The wealth and diversity of the visual arts in Wales in the 20th century is nowhere more evident than in the artists' collections of graphic art acquired since 1986. On a visit to some of America's major photographic collections in 1984, Alistair Crawford discovered the benefits of housing in one place collections representing individual artists. The University has never had the funds to buy expensive single works of art, nor does it see this as its role. Artists' collections however, as the American institutions demonstrated, offered great potential for research. In some instances artists have been asked to select the works by which they are to be represented for posterity - works which they consider significant in their development as artists. Copies of archive material, press reviews, diaries and a photographic record of works have also been made available. The University actively seeks to acquire collections, negotiating excellent terms with the generous co-operation of the artist or their families; there have also been numerous gifts included with the formation of artists' collections. Furthermore, such collections offer excellent value for money; the George Chapman, John Elwyn, Handel Evans, Rigby Graham and Keith Vaughan collections were all acquired with the invaluable support of the Victoria and Albert Museum/Museum and Galleries Commission Purchase Fund which has effectively doubled the University's purchasing power. (The first artists' collections acquired are recorded under photography.)

The 27 lithographs and screenprints by Eric Malthouse (b.1914) purchased in 1986 represents the work of one of the few printmakers working in Wales in the 1950s and 1960s - it is the largest group of his works in a public collection. Malthouse trained at Birmingham School of Art and moved to Cardiff in 1944 to teach at the College of Art. He subsequently featured prominently in Wales as a prolific painter and active exhibitor, and as a founder member of the 56 Group Wales. The prints which span the years 1956 to 1972 take us on a journey from his last days of figuration (*Sorting Fish, St Ives* 1956) through his increasing involvement with abstraction including *Façade* (1969), screenprints made after his designs for John Dankworth's performance of Sir William Walton's music based on Edith Sitwell's poems of the same title, and nine *Prynu Dol* (1970) screenprints inspired by the writings of Kate Roberts.

Hugh Blaker (1873-1936) *Boy with a Rope* pencil and charcoal c.1900

Handel Evans (b.1932) *The Vaults* tempera 1987

George Chapman (1908-1993) *The First Building* etching 1960

Rigby Graham (b.1931) *Homage to Cavafy* woodcut 1987

Keith Vaughan (1912-77) *Festival Dancers* lithograph 1951

The graphic works by Handel Evans (b.1932) in the collection are a result of the policy to assemble small retrospective collections representing individual artists from or working in Wales. Five drawings and tempera paintings on paper were purchased from the artist in 1990 covering the period in his career 1951-1987 - all were chosen from a book published on his work in Germany in 1989. Evans trained at Cardiff College of Art 1949-54 and has since made a living as a practising artist, travelling widely and spending much of his time in the Caribbean and Germany where he now lives; his reputation is greatest in Germany and America. *A Game of Dice, Paris* (1951) was produced as a student at Cardiff, The Vaults (1987) represents his long-standing involvement with abstraction, whilst *The Actor's Dream* 1987 signifies his return to figurative painting. *The Resurrection* (1960), a proposed mural for a Welsh chapel, was given by the artist in 1990 and *Limbs* (1985) was donated to the collection by Alan Soons of the USA in 1995.

John Elwyn's paintings of the Cardiganshire landscape have found widespread appeal, though his life class and self portrait drawings were virtually unknown until they were exhibited for the first time at the School of Art in 1996. The 111 drawings spanning the years 1936 to 1966 provide a unique opportunity to observe the artist's development and maturity in the life class - as a student at Carmarthen and the Royal College of Art, and instructor in the life classes at Portsmouth and Winchester Schools of Art. John Elwyn (b.1916) was a product of the British art school system which believed that drawing the human figure was the best means to test an artist's powers of observation and expression. The informal drawings he made of the model glimpsed between the backs of his students at Winchester, together with the spontaneous studies in chalk, are in marked contrast to the early academic drawings. John Elwyn's feeling for the natural rhythm of the pose, his consummate technical ability as a draughtsman and his versatility in a wide range of media places him firmly in the classic European figurative tradition. In addition to the purchase, John Elwyn has donated ten lithographs, three drawings of himself by others, and his portrait in oil of *Dennis William Reed* (1947).

George Chapman (1908-1993) first painted the villages that comprise the south Wales coal-mining valleys in 1953, the same year that he began etching. There followed a period of considerable success - highly praised solo exhibitions in London with extensive press and media coverage. In the etchings, such as *The Rhondda Suite* commissioned by St George's Gallery Prints, London in 1960, Chapman's strong sense of graphic design is most evident; he revelled in the patterns made by the telegraph poles and wires, the television aerials, the pit-head winding gear and chimney stacks, the railway signals and the herringbone roofs of the steep terraced miners' houses. The first group of 27 etchings was purchased from the artist in 1986; 23 etchings, posters and drawings followed in 1988; 15 etchings in 1991; seven in 1992; and several individual purchases from London galleries now form what is believed to be a complete set of his etchings. Chapman's pictures of the Rhondda Valley are a visual novel of the people of the mining communities and their homes; they convey the spirit of an industrial community that has long since changed and as such are important historical records of the industrial face of Wales.

Rigby Graham's work also exhibits a concern to portray particular aspects of the landscape and convey a vision of their significance beyond ordinary appearance. In Graham's vision these particulars are to be found in the 'mundane' details of litter, street furniture, factory machinery, weeds and all aspects of the landscape normally kept on the periphery of vision. Neglect and dereliction, ruin and change are constant themes. The 46 lithographs from Graham's *Leicestershire* published in 1980, seven prints and four drawings by Rigby Graham (b.1931) purchased in 1985 includes the first acquisition of artists' working drawings. Graham is an immensely prolific and versatile painter, printmaker and designer, and has illustrated hundreds of books for private and commercial presses. He works firmly within the British landscape tradition, extending the neo-romantic themes of Sutherland, Minton and Vaughan; his work not only broadens the scope of post-war neo-romanticism in the collection but also resonates with its origins in the etchings of Palmer, Sutherland, Drury et al. As a printmaker he has worked in wood and lino cut, lithography, monoprint and to a lesser degree etching. The 20 large colour woodcuts, editioned by Goldmark Gallery in Rutland, demonstrate Graham's attachment to the Romantic aspects of other localities in England and Wales, as well as Malta, Germany, Italy and Greece. Prints such as *Flughafen, Hannover* (1986), *Venice - The Birds* (1987), *Grand Canal, Venice* (1987) and *Homage to Cavafy* (1987), bear witness to his technical versatility, bold use of colour, instinctive sense of design, the confidence of his draughtsmanship and his immense commitment and energy. This latter acquisition was made possible through the generosity of Goldmark Gallery.

Keith Vaughan (1912-1977) emerged in the 1950s as the foremost exponent of neo-romanticism in England. In 1985 Crawford negotiated with the Executors of the Vaughan Estate for the purchase of the complete set of 41 original pen and ink illustrations for PH Newby's *The Spirit of Jem* (1947), 69 photographs and 363 items of printed ephemera, proofs, magazine advertisements, book jackets etc. that formed Vaughan's personal archive of his output as an illustrator and graphic designer. Of particular significance is *Dick's Book of Photos* (1939), 34 photographs compiled by Vaughan in a hand-made album, recording one idyllic summer on the beach at Pagham on the eve of war, dedicated to his brother Richard who was killed in action in 1940. There are also 35 photographs of the *Ballet Russe de Monte Carlo*, taken around 1933 but relevant later in his career as a source for paintings. A group of early linocuts, six lithographs (he is known to have made only 8-10 lithographs) and a monoprint from the 1940s have subsequently been purchased to broaden the scope of the Vaughan collection.

Edgar Holloway (b.1916) was a key figure in the etching revival of the 1930s, he was one of the very few artists not to turn their back on etching after the market collapsed. By the age of twenty, he had been given two solo exhibitions in London, his work had been purchased by the V&A and the British Museum, and T. S. Eliot, Stephen Spender and Herbert Read were among the many who sat for him for their portraits. In 1949, he joined the Guild of St Joseph and St Dominic on Ditchling Common established by Eric Gill working solely in graphic design until 1969 when his interest in etching was rekindled. Holloway's etchings and engravings form a visual diary of his family, friends and travels - and include a remarkable series of etched self portraits made between 1930 and 1995. His *Self Portrait No.6* was purchased by Sidney Greenslade in 1934, but the opportunity to acquire 14 more Holloway etchings representing the intervening years did not arise until Robert Meyrick was invited to curate a national travelling exhibition of his work in 1994.

Hugh Blaker (1873-1936) is best remembered for his role as art advisor to the Davies sisters, only one of many roles he took on throughout his life; he was at times painter, writer, critic, philosopher, actor, museum curator, art dealer and collector. He received a privileged art education in Paris, Antwerp and England. On Blaker's death his paintings and drawings passed to his sister Jane at Gregynog where they remained in storage until they were transferred to Aberystwyth in June 1990 as part of the Gregynog Loan. The collection of 127 works on paper includes academic life drawings of the 1890s, 12 original pen and ink illustrations, and his later experiments with Modernism in the 1910s. Blaker's desire to experiment and to be 'modern' led him in many unexpected directions, these especially provide a fascinating insight into the creative output of a truly 'modern' individual who, through his role in the formation of the Davies Collection of Impressionist paintings, played a significant part in the development of the history of art in Wales.

Ivor Williams (1908-1982), son of the Maesteg-born painter Christopher Williams, inherited his father's aptitude for portraiture and large-scale figure compositions. In later years he devoted much of his time to large religious subjects. *The Healing of the Sick of the Palsy* (1951-54), measuring 7 x 9 ¼ ft, was the first of Williams' large biblical compositions on the theme of the universal teachings of Christ, of sickness and healing and faith triumphant. The painting is composed of thirty individual portraits of family, neighbours and friends. The artist attempted to create a painting that was `timeless'; costumes are ancient and modern, and people of different races and ages are juxtaposed deliberately to emphasise Williams' belief that Christ speaks to all ages and regardless of the colour of their skin. In 1962 Williams loaned the painting to the Church of St Martin-in-the-fields, London where it remained for over twenty years before it was returned to his studio in Cardiff. In 1993 the artist's family offered the painting to the University, with fifty-six life drawings and studies for paintings from his Slade School days, and fourteen oil paintings, mostly portraits, spanning the artist's career.

The teaching and research potential has been the primary consideration in the acquisition of all artists' collections. National touring exhibitions with catalogues using material from the Hugh Blaker, George Chapman, John Elwyn and Edgar Holloway collections have already taken place, thus re-affirming the School of Art's commitment to art in Wales. It is another example of the policy to develop collections of national importance; a valuable resource for future generations of students and scholars. **RM**

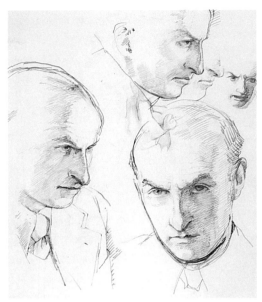

John Elwyn (b.1916) *Self Portrait Studies* pencil 1950s

Ivor Williams (1908-82) *Christ Healing the Sick of the Palsy* oil 1951-4

Eric Malthouse (b.1914) *First Façade Suite IV* screenprint 1969

Augustus John (1878-1961) *Miss Gwendoline John - Lady in a Hat* etching and drypoint 1902

Percy Wyndham Lewis (1884-1957) *Woman Standing* pencil 1910s

James McNeill Whistler (1834-1957) *The Traghetto (First Venice Set)* etching 1880

the Gregynog Loan

The University's collection of prints has been immeasurably enhanced since the Gregynog Loan was deposited in Aberystwyth in 1989. Pioneers of the 'Print Revival' in Britain such as James McNeill Whistler, Augustus John, William Strang and D Y Cameron were hitherto notable omissions in the collection.

Acquired by Gwendolen and Margaret Davies between about 1908 and 1932, their print collection included works which had personal associations for them as well as those which represented some of the finest achievements in printmaking in Britain and on the Continent over the past five hundred years. There are the prints by artists with whom they were acquainted: Hugh Blaker, his friend John Whitcombe (1872-1918), curator of the Victoria Art Gallery, Bath and a particularly fine group of etchings by the Welsh artist Fred Richards given to the sisters by Thomas Jones. As one might expect there is a fair representation of contemporary French printmaking including work by Auguste Brouet (1872-1941), Jean Louis Forain (1852-1931), Alphonse Legros (1837-1911), Auguste Lepère (1849-1918) and Pierre Auguste Renoir (1841-1919). British etchers at the turn of the century, however, are less well represented although Frank Brangwyn (1867-1956) and David Young Cameron (1865-1945) are represented by individual etchings and there are four prints by the Scottish etcher William Strang (1859-1921).

The sisters subscribed to the Print Collectors' Club, which was established in 1921, and in return received a limited edition presentation print annually; works by Stanley Anderson (1884-1966), Alfred Bentley (1879-1923), Gerald Brockhurst, Malcolm Osborne (1880-1963), Raymond Ray-Jones (1886-1942) and William Walcot (1874-1943) were acquired in this way. The closest they came to 'serious' print collecting, at a time when it was not only fashionable but highly profitable to do so, is in the important group of prints they acquired by eminent European masters: five engravings by Albrecht Dürer (1471-1538), three etchings by Rembrandt van Rijn (1606-1669), eight etchings by the Swedish artist Anders Zorn (1860-1920) and twenty-five etchings and lithographs by James McNeill Whistler. There are eighty-four etchings by Augustus John (1878-1961) who was already a well established painter when Gwendoline Davies, persuaded by Blaker, purchased this set, along with 'numerous drawings', from an exhibition of John's prints at the Chenil Gallery, London in 1919. Hugh Blaker had been a long-time admirer of John's work, indeed he had twenty-eight examples in his own collection.

The Davies sisters' prints, like their 'Old Masters' and 18th-19th British paintings appear to have been acquired less methodically than the paintings and sculpture they purchased to represent the development of art in 19th-century France, mostly on the recommendation of their advisor Hugh Blaker. It became clear very early on that the sisters intended leaving their collection of French art to the Nation and in many ways this decision 'to buy for posterity' was reflected in their choice of works and the manner in which they were acquired to extend the scope of the collection.

In 1952 Margaret Davies donated the Dürer engravings, Rembrandt etchings and two prints by Anders Zorn to the National Library of Wales. In addition she presented Whistler's *Thames Set* in memory of her step-mother Mrs Edward Davies, 57 etchings by Augustus John and five by Jean Louis Forain in memory of her sister Gwendoline. The remainder of the prints, framed on walls or for the most part mounted in portfolios, passed to the University of Wales along with Gregynog and its contents in 1963. These prints came to Aberystwyth on long-term loan in 1989 together with 132 watercolours and drawings. These are principally by Hugh Blaker (who is included here under *Artists' Collections*), but there are also watercolours by D Murray Smith (1865-1952) and a pencil drawing of a standing female by Percy Wyndham Lewis (1884-1957), which had formerly belonged to Hugh Blaker. Re-uniting the Davies sisters' prints in the University and the National Library of Wales for the first time in over 40 years, Robert Meyrick curated 'Gregynog Prints', a major exhibition which toured nationally between 1994 and 1997. **RM**

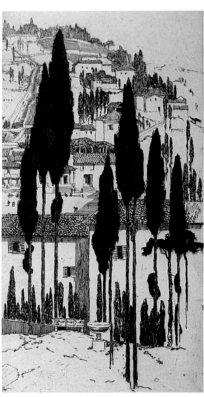

Frederick Richards (1878-1932) *Fiesole - near Florence No.11* etching 1916

contemporary collecting: Photography

Elio Ciol (b.1929) *Muri di S.Damiano, Assisi* photograph 1967

The decision to form a collection of photographs within the continuing history and development of printmaking came at a time when many British museums and galleries were still coming to terms with the notion of photography as an art form. The 1970s had witnessed an unprecedented interest in the history and practice of photography - from private galleries, public museums and publishers. Alistair Crawford took the American museums as a model for the Aberystwyth collection. In 1984 he had visited the principal collections of photography in museums and universities in New York, Austin, Tucson, San Francisco, Los Angeles and Chicago. Aberystwyth was then the only British university offering undergraduate and postgraduate practical and art history courses in photography. A teaching and research collection, however, did not exist in the University; there was a Victorian album of 60 albumen photographs depicting travels in Europe and north Africa attributed to Felice Beato, James Robertson and others, and also a single photograph acquired as part of the Gulbenkian Loan Scheme in 1968. *Sand Form Albion* by Raymond Moore (1920-88) was purchased from an Arts Council touring exhibition. The photographs that have since been acquired represent contemporary practice in Britain, Italy and Wales.

The National Library of Wales in Aberystwyth holds extensive collections of early Welsh photography, but at the time the University's photography collection began to be developed there was no policy at the Library to collect either the work of contemporary photographers in Wales or photography as art. The first significant group of contemporary Welsh photography was bought in 1986; it included the work of John Blakemore (b.1936), Jeffrey Morgan, John Nesbitt, Leslie Price (b.1938) and William Tsui. The University's holdings of post-war photography in Wales, however, consists principally of bodies of work by individual artists, and a small number of photographs by British photographers shown in Wales - David Bailey, Paul Hill, Angus McBean and Lord Snowdon, demonstrate the breadth of contemporary photography practice. The first collection acquired from a Welsh photographer was that of Gwyn Martin (b.1921) purchased in 1986. Born in the Rhondda, Martin trained as a pharmacist and from 1948 became a partner in Taylor Lloyd Ltd, his father-in-law's chemist shop in Aberystwyth. The 77 photographs of Aberystwyth and its environs taken between 1956 and 1986 are a record of his home town and its community. Rudy Lewis (b.1939), on the other hand, has lived and worked in Aberystwyth all his life yet has consistently found his subject on the other side of the world - on his travels to Bolivia, Tibet, China, Japan *et al. The Holy Man, Rajasthan, Nepal, Massai Woman, Amboseli, Kenya and Child* and *Buddha, Nepal* at first seem familiar - women and children,

Carlo Bevilacqua (1900-88) *Friends on Sunday* photograph 1981

Mario Giacomelli (b.1925) *Scanno* photograph 1955-9

Guiseppe Cavalli (1904-61) *Natura Morta* photograph 1950s

Keith Vaughan (1912-77) *Lotus Eater* from *Dick's Book of Photos* photograph 1939

Angus McBean (1904-90) *Audrey Hepburn* photograph 1949/86

people going about their daily business - yet on closer inspection are simultaneously about 'strangeness' and 'difference'. A collection of 58 photographs by Lewis was purchased from his solo exhibition at Aberystwyth Arts Centre in 1991. In 1989 Ron Davies (b.1921), a freelance photographer for press and television, donated 28 photographs of the landscape and people of Wales from his book *Llun a Chân* (1983) and in 1995 he gave 100 photographs illustrating a day in the life of the National Colliery, Porth in 1959. These now compliment Leslie Price's series of photographs of the coal miners' national strike in 1984 purchased in 1991. *Old College, Aberystwyth* (1979) by Robert Greetham, who became first Director of Ffotogallery in Cardiff, was the first acquisition in the formation of a collection of student photographs which has grown steadily since 1979 with examples selected from annual degree exhibitions.

The outstanding collection of Italian post-war photographs has been built up by Alistair Crawford who, during his time at Aberystwyth, has gained an international reputation as a photographic historian. Through contacts established on personal research projects he has negotiated for Aberystwyth important collections of work by several eminent 20th-century Italian photographers. Touring exhibitions and scholarly catalogues by Crawford introduced their work to the British public for the first time.

Elio Ciol (b.1929) was the first photographer with whom Crawford made contact. In 1977 he mounted an exhibition of Ciol's photographs that toured nine venues in the UK. Ciol was born in Friuli and at fifteen began his life-long career as a photographer in his father's photography business. He has published over a hundred photography books on different aspects of Italian society and culture. Much of Ciol's energies have gone into building up a photographic archive of Italian works of art and architecture, particularly in the mountainous provinces of northern Italy. Many of his books have been sponsored by private patrons, commerce, industry and the church, all of whom share an interest in the culture and identity of the region and the society whose way of life and language are under threat. A collection of 66 photographs by Ciol was purchased in 1986 representing the range of Ciol's oeuvre; documentary, social and environmental studies of Italy, Kenya, Egypt, Turkey and Wales.

In 1983 Crawford organised a retrospective exhibition of photographs by Mario Giacomelli (b.1925) for Ffotogallery, Cardiff which toured Britain and Ireland. Giacomelli, born in Senegallia, near Urbino, is Italy's foremost contemporary photographer, his reputation is international and his work is represented in public collections throughout the world. The 135 photographs by Giacomelli acquired for Aberystwyth in 1986 is surpassed in its size and scope only by the University of Parma. The collection forms a retrospective survey of Giacomelli's career from early 'art' photography to his discovery of the camera's potential for social and political comment. It also charts thematic progressions from landscape subjects and the transfiguration of the landscape by humans, to his potent depictions of old age and death. *The Beginning* (1955), *Nudes* (1956-60), *Lourdes* (1957), *Scanno* (1955-9) *On Becoming Aware of Nature* (1977-80) and *Do not Ask me Questions* (1981) demonstrate his preference for working in series of photographs; meaning accumulates when the images are viewed consecutively. This cinematic concept paralleled the contemporary Neo-Realist films of Rossellini and Visconti in post-war Italy.

The 72 photographs by Carlo Bevilacqua (1900-1988) purchased in 1986 illustrate his development from a leading exponent of European Pictorialism to more documentary 'aesthetic' salon photography in the post-war period. After it was acquired for the university the collection formed Bevilacqua's first solo exhibition; 'Carlo Bevilacqua - Il Maestro' showed at Aberystwyth in November 1987 then toured nationally. Bevilacqua, who like Ciol was from the Friuli region, began taking photographs in about 1942 and he quickly became a seminal influence on other photographers working in northern Italy through his involvement with many of the region's photographic societies, including *La Gondola*, the group founded by Paolo Monti. He contributed to numerous Salon exhibitions around the world, picking up many international photography awards and, in 1955, he was elected member of the International Federation of Photographic Art. The photographs in the collection were selected to illustrate his extensive range of graphic techniques. Starkly contrasting and near abstract images like *(Man walking past barbed wire) Caorle* (c.1958), or the carefully structured *White Frame* (c.1955) with its subtle range of pale greys through to whites (espousing Giuseppe Cavalli's preference for the formal aesthetic qualities over the subject itself), clearly establish him as a darkroom virtuoso, demonstrating absolute control in the manipulation of the image during the printing process.

In 1990 a unique opportunity presented itself to acquire from the private collection of an Italian photographer and photographic historian a rare group of vintage prints by many of the key exponents in the history of Italian photography from c.1910 to the 1960s, all of whom by then had died. The collection not only consolidated the University's existing holdings of Italian photography but also served to explain and contextualise the work of Bevilacqua, Ciol and Giacomelli, and at the same time strengthen the importance of the collection outside of Italy. There were six photographs by each of Guiseppe Cavalli (1904-61) and Paolo Monti (1908-82), five by Ferrucio Leiss (1896-1967), and four socio-documentary photographs by Toni del Tin (1915-1973). The Cavalli's are of particular importance in demonstrating his enormous influence upon 'art' photographers in Italy. In 1993, a further collection was purchased from the same source; seven more photographs by each of Cavalli and del Tin, five by Monti, 15 by Leiss and new to the collection were eight prints by Vicenzo Balocchi (1892-1957), two by Carlo Matis and one each by Luigi Veronesi (b.1908), Gualberto Davolio-Marani, Italo Bertoglio and Fulvio Roiter (b.1926). The scope of the Italian collection has since been broadened by the acquisition of 46 works by the Italian photographer Roberto Salbitani (b.1945) and 25 by Priamo Tolu (b.1937) selected from an exhibition of his photographs of Uganda and his native Sardinia curated by the School of Art in 1995. Aberystwyth now holds the most important collection of post-war Italian photography outside of Italy. **RM**

contemporary collecting: Ceramics

In 1971 Moira Vincentelli, a newly appointed Tutor in Art History, assumed responsibility from David Tinker for the ceramics collection. At the time there was no available funding for the care or display of the existing collections, dispersed as they were throughout the University and Moira Vincentelli's first step was to undertake an inventory. Tinker's plan to "sell to reinforce" certain aspects of the collection was put into practice with the sale of a group of netsukes. This was carried out on the understanding that the income was used to re-establish a purchase fund to collect post-war British and Welsh studio ceramics, illustrating developments since the Sidney Greenslade's last purchases in 1935. Part of the proceeds of the sales funded the purchase of display cases to exhibit a small selection of the ceramics and the remainder enabled collecting to recommence on a limited scale. The first purchases included works by Michael Casson, Alan Caiger Smith and Gordon Baldwin. In 1970, the early studio pottery had been moved to the store of the newly opened Great Hall Gallery where it was proposed they would be put on show in rotation.

In March 1975 the Welsh Arts Council (WAC) and the Craft Advisory Committee matched the funds raised by the proceeds of the sale with a substantial grant to catalogue and display the ceramic collection. In that year the potter Michael Casson was invited by the WAC to give his professional opinion of the collection. Such was the Committee's high regard for the collection of early studio pottery that he was asked by the Crafts Committee of the WAC to put forward the names of potters in or from Wales whose work in his opinion would contribute to the existing holdings. The WAC gave a Commission Award for a number of contemporary potters to produce works for the collection including Patrick Adamson, David Frith, Trefor Owen, Peter Starkey and Terry Bell Hughes. The WAC also donated two pieces of Ruskin Pottery made at Smethwick in William Howson Taylor's art pottery works and previously unrepresented in the collection.

In August 1975 the International Ceramics Symposium, an annual event founded in 1963 by Professor Kurt Ohnsorg in Austria, was held in Cardiff for one month under the auspices of Cardiff College of Art to provide 'informal practical working situations ... in an intensely creative atmosphere'. The delegates from Britain, America, west and eastern Europe, Ireland and Turkey, were brought to visit the collection and each eventually deposited a work produced at the Symposium for the University. Among the work donated to the collection were large scale pieces by the Japanese potter Kempei Nakamura, a series of works by European potters such as Marianne Rahneberg (6), Lillimar Peterson (5), Illona Benko (7) Anton Raidel (4), Marta Taberyova (3) and from the British potters Mary White (20), Alan Barrett-Danes (2), Tony Franks (3) and Francis Woodley (3). The Cardiff Symposium gift formed the first exhibition in the new display cases in 1976. Larger cases were purchased to put on small changing displays from the collection. In 1978 the Crafts Advisory Council bought and presented ceramics by Lucie Rie, David Leach and Alan Barrett-Danes.

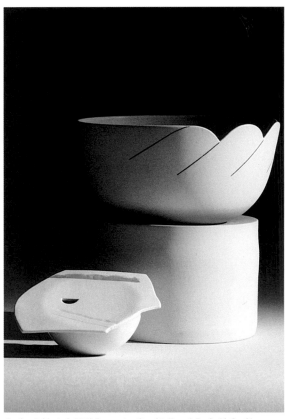

Gordon Baldwin (b.1932) *Fragment as Complete Form & Bowl with Graphics* porcelain 1974

Anna Noel (b.1958) *Cat and Tiger* raku 1986

Megume Oiwake, vase and dish, slip-decorated earthenware 1991

Hans Coper (1920-81) stoneware vessel & Lucie Rie (1902-95) bottle with flared rim, porcelain 1970s

Deidre Daw 'Chrisopher Columbus...' earthenware 1992

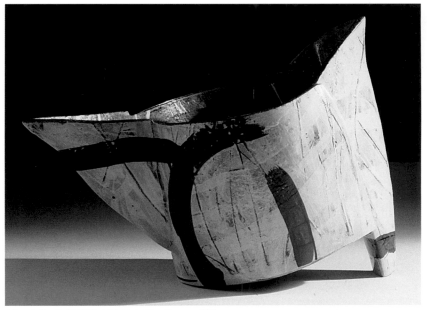

Alison Britton (b.1948) *Tilted Pot* slab-built earthenware 1990

The reinstatement of the acquisition of ceramics was paralleled with the dispersal of other parts of the collection: pottery from Professor John Garstang's excavations in Jericho in 1931-33, to which the University had subscribed, was transferred to Department of Archaeology of Birmingham City Museum and Art Gallery in 1973 to join the bulk of Gartstang's excavations already there, this was in exchange for several Egyptian, Greek, Roman and Middle Eastern pots as historical examples to complement the remaining holdings in Aberystwyth.

Active collecting coincided with an upturn in the popularity of studio ceramics, the growth of ceramics exhibitions and increased coverage in new publications such as *Ceramic Review*, established by the Craft Potters Association in 1970 and in *Crafts* magazine, started by the Crafts Advisory Committee in 1973 (later to become the Crafts Council in 1979). Many ceramicists produced work which questioned the categories and boundaries of art and craft and claimed ground for the sculptural and conceptual in ceramics. In April 1974, in addition to works aligned with traditional functional ware - by David Leach, Eileen Lewenstein, Alan Caiger Smith and Michael Casson - three porcelain sculptural pieces by Gordon Baldwin were purchased from the Craftsmen Artists' Association at the British Crafts Centre including *Fragment as Complete Form* and *Bowl on a Base with Graphics*. A layered bowl on a narrow foot by Sheila Fournier purchased in 1975 and Glenys Barton's *Sky Plateau II*, produced during a residency at the Wedgwood factory and purchased in 1978, also declare their right to continue a tradition of contemplative and emphatically non-utilitarian ceramic forms.

Although the acquisition policy has always put great emphasis on the purchase of works by contemporary artists there have been acquisitions of work produced during the dormant period of the collection, particularly when the working life of a potter has continued in the interim; hence the purchase in 1976 of a 'Pilgrim plate' (c.1973) by Bernard Leach; a stoneware jar (c.1962) by Michael Cardew made in Abuja, Africa and bought in 1974, and a Denise Wren vase decorated with a Celtic design, influenced by her training with the designer Archibald Knox, acquired from an auction at Christies in 1988. Occasionally generous gifts have performed the same function, most notably those made in 1985 and 1988 by Lady Pamela Glenconner, a founding figure of the Craft Potters Association, which included works by potters such as Katharine Pleydell-Bouverie, Helen Pincombe, Dennis Moore, Ray Finch, Alan Caiger Smith, Colin Pearson and Rosemary Wren. There have been many other individual gifts from institutions, collectors and potters which have greatly enriched the collection: the Crafts Advisory Committee gave a sculptural work by Graham Burr in 1980 and in 1991 its descendant the Crafts Council loaned three pieces by Elizabeth Fritsch; in 1989 David Whiting gave three pots by his father Geoffrey Whiting; in 1990 gallery owner Michael O'Brien donated a bowl by Ladi Kwali, a renowned pupil of Michael Cardew in Abuja, and in the same year the potter Sebastian Blackie gave one of his own paper-fired, hand built vessels. More recently, in 1995 a local artist and collector Mabel Packenham Walsh gave seven items of ceramics including works by Glenys Barton and John Maltby and one of her own paintings. In 1996 the potter Peter Beard donated one of his own pots to the collection from a Ceramic Series exhibition in Aberystwyth Arts Centre, and Phil Rogers working in Rhayder has also presented his own works to the collection.

The *Ceramics Series* exhibitions, begun by the Arts Centre in 1982, have been showcases of the best of contemporary potters. Purchases have been made from over forty of these exhibitions which have promoted work by the foremost contemporary potters: Richard Batterham, Mary Bennett, Clive Bowen, David Frith, Jane Hamlyn, Ewen Henderson, Wally Keeler, Richard Launder, Sidig El Nigoumi, Jaqui Poncelet, Phil Rogers, Janice Tchalenko and so on - representing the diversity of contemporary practice from 'ethical' utilitarian pots in the Leach tradition to experimental and conceptual pieces. The Elvet Lewis Bequest in 1980 provided a considerable boost to the acquisition and display facilities. By 1986 the first phase of the Ceramic Gallery in Aberystwyth Arts Centre was completed followed by phase two in 1987 and phase three in 1988. As a consequence all the early studio pottery collection was put on permanent view as 'visible storage'; this now complements both temporary exhibitions from the collections and touring exhibitions organised by the Arts Centre in the rest of the gallery. Again, many pots have been purchased from these exhibitions including a group of 12 items of contemporary Japanese ceramics from *Thought For Food* in July 1991 - works by Mashahiro Mori, Shiro Otani, Megumi Oiwake, Tetsuo Hirakawa, Takehito Takeda, Chieko Yorigame, Ryoji Koie and Katsue Ibata which resonate with both the early studio pottery and its concern with Chinese and Japanese forms and glazes, and with the smaller amount of oriental pottery that was purchased by Greenslade in the inter-war years from dealers in London. Many more works have been purchased from touring exhibitions in the Arts Centre and further afield - from *In the First Place: an exhibition of craft from Wales* in August 1990 (works by Beverley Bell-Hughes, Terry Bell-Hughes, Jo Duncalf, Joanna Mallin Davies, Julie Goldstone, Gwen Heeney, Anna Noel and Simon Smith); from the *New Spirit* exhibition in 1989 (pieces by Fiona Salazar & Christine Constant); from *Free Spirits* at Llantarnam Grange, Monmouthshire in 1990 (pots by Sheila Casson, Sandy Brown, Betty Blandino and Jane Staniland); from *The American Way* at Aberystwyth Arts Centre in July 1994, (works by American ceramicists Bruce Wynn, Ann Agee, Dierde Daw, Mark Pharis and Annabeth Rosen).

Another source of acquisition has been the International Potters Festival, organised by the North and South Wales Potters' Associations and Aberystwyth Arts Centre and held biennally at Aberystwyth since 1987. Works by the participating artists were purchased: Mick Casson, Mike Dodd, Karin Hessenberg, Walter Keeler, Archie McColl, Jeff Mincham (Australia), Angus Suttie, Takeshi Yasuda, Greg Daly (Australia), Ulla Viotti (Sweden) Aage Birck (Denmark). The opportunity to purchase works from European potters has been followed up in the ensuing Festivals: Gerhild Tschachler Nagy (Austria), Gabriella Nepo Steindorf (Austria), Claudi Casanovas (Spain), Asibe Iddo and Asabe Magasi (Africa). In later Festivals the acquisition of European ceramics has continued with works by Gabriele Koch (Germany and UK), Tula Elieson (Norway) and Václav Serák (Czechoslovakia). Visits by Moira Vincentelli to various other festivals have also resulted in purchases; at the Oslo International Ceramics Symposium in 1989 she acquired ceramics by Barbara Brown (USA) and Sandra Johnstone (USA); nearer to home at the Northern potters camps at Bretton Hall (1990) and Ripon (1991) works by Patrick Sargent (Switzerland and UK), Rita Ternes (Germany), Thomas Naethe (Germany), Peter Meanley and Paul Scott were acquired. Much of the work collected at these events has been backed up with audio and video-taped lectures, demonstrations and interviews with potters which are added to the Ceramic Archive, the project of a personal research interest of Moira Vincentelli initiated with the gift of the Craftsmen Potters' Association Archive in 1987. The project is affiliated to the activities of the ceramics collection and flourishes with support from the Council of Museums in Wales and the Arts Council of Wales.

Even with the greatly increased funding some ceramics, such as the work of Hans Coper and Lucie Rie are beyond the financial scope of the collection and it is only through funding bodies such as the Victoria & Albert Museum/Museums and Galleries Commission Grant in Aid fund and the National Art Collections Fund that such purchases can be considered. These funds have enabled the purchase of works by many internationally renowned ceramicists; Paul Soldner (V&A/MGC) in 1987; Ewan Henderson *Skull Mountain* in 1988; Vladimir Tsivin (Russia) *Silenus,* made during a residency at South Glamorgan Institute, in 1990 (NACF & V&A); Alison Britton *Tilted Pot* (V&A/MGC) in 1991; Richard Slee *Torch* and *Leaf* from a *Ceramic Series* exhibition in 1992 (NACF, V&A/MGC).

The most significant purchase made with the aid of NACF and V&A/MGC funding has been the group of 25 ceramics selected from the collection of the late David Hines (1921-1992) shortly before his death, comprising works by Dierdre Burnett (1), Joanna Constandinidis (2), Hans Coper (1), Ray Finch (1), Karin Hessenberg (1), Ann James (1), David Leach (3), Eileen Lewenstein (1), Mary Rogers (4), Lucie Rie (4), John Ward (4), Geoffrey Whiting (1) and Po Chap Yeap (1). David Hines became involved in the ceramics industry through the family business of industrial potters' merchants. He collected paintings and ceramics from an early age and during the 1950s began acquiring Swedish ceramics from the Gustavsberg Factory. He started to acquire contemporary British potters' work in the 1960s, the majority of which he bought from the Peter Dingley Gallery in Stratford-upon-Avon. Hines responded to the tactile and visual impact of a pot, it had to be 'a joy to hold and handle'. After his retirement from the family business he became actively involved with the National Arts Collection Fund. This selection, made by Moira Vincentelli and his wife Shirley Hines, is representative of British ceramics during the 1970s and 1980s and contains the work of potters new to the collection - Hans Coper, Mary Rogers, John Ward and Po Chap Yeap. In purchasing this group rather than individual pieces it has been possible to retain something of the character of Hines' original collection.

The University continues to collect work representative of the 'two strands' of studio ceramics production - the so-called 'ethical pot' of the Leach tradition (utile, democratic, ego-less, craft) and the 'modernist' pots (self-conscious, non-functional, experimental, art) perceived to be direct descendants, through their work and teaching, of Staite Murray and post-war potters, particularly Lucie Rie and Hans Coper. The University is one of the few museums in Britain that has collected studio ceramics from outside the UK. Significantly the lacuna in the collection is work produced during the period from 1936 to 1974, a large gap to 'fill' but then the collection has never laid claim to be a 'universal survey' of the history of studio ceramics. Even so the existing holdings, through the selection made by Moira Vincentelli over the last 'two strands', admirably documents the changing nature of the debates between the makers of ceramic artefacts; what becomes apparent through the collection is that the 'two strands' above are not mutually exclusive, that if 'tradition' is invoked, ceramic history contains precedents for all manner of approaches. **NH**

Paul Soldner (b.1921) *Large vessel*, raku stoneware 1987

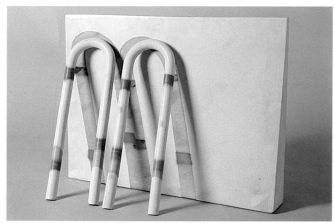

Graham Burr (b.1929) Flat form with three leaning arches, porcelain 1980

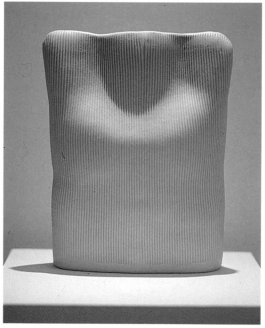

Vladimir Tsivin (b.1949) *Silenus* porcelain with chamotte 1990

Paddy Adamson (b.1944) Lizard lidded pot, stoneware 1976

The Edward Davies Building (opened 1907)

The collections today

Select Bibliography

Crawford, Alistair *The Print Collection of the University College of Wales, Aberystwyth* **Visual Art Department, UCW Aberystwyth 1984**

Evans, Ruth *John Williams 1840-1926* **University of Wales Press Cardiff 1952**

Jones, Thomas *A Welsh Broth* **W Griffiths & Co., The Cambrian News Ltd., Abersytwyth 1950**

Jones, Thomas *A Diary with Letters 1931-1950*, **Oxford University Press, London 1954**

Meyrick, Robert *Gregynog Prints* **UWA School of Art Press Aberystwyth 1994**

Morgan, Iwan J (ed) *The College by the Sea* **The Students' Representative Council and The College Council, The Cambrian News Ltd., Aberystwyth 1928**

Vincentelli, Moira 'The U C W Museum and Art Collections 1872-1918' *Ceredigion, Journal of the Ceredigion Antiquarian Society* 1979 **pp389-403**

Vincentelli, Moira 'The U C W Arts and Crafts Museum' *Ceredigion, Journal of the Ceredigion Antiquarian Society* 1980 **pp42-52**

Vincentelli, Moira & Hale, Anna *A Catalogue of Early Studio Pottery in the Collections of the University College of Wales, Aberystwyth* **UCW Aberystwyth 1986**

Vincentelli, Moira *The Ceramic Collection* **UWA School of Art Press 1993**

George Powell's correspondence has been deposited by the University in the National Library of Wales, Aberystwyth

Calendars of the University College of Wales, Abersytwyth and *Reports to the Court of Governors* **1874-1996**

the Edward Davies Building

At the turn of the century the University had outgrown its original premises on the seafront and was seeking ways of re-housing some of its departments. Chemistry was a rapidly expanding research department in desperate need of additional accommodation when in March 1903 Gwendoline, Margaret and David Davies, and their step-mother Mrs Edward Davies, offered £20,000 towards the cost of new laboratories in memory of their father Edward Davies who had died in 1898.

An eleven acre site on Buarth Mawr was purchased for £2,500 from Colonel W H Colby, a member of Council. Professor J J Sudborough, then Professor of Chemistry, travelled the UK and to Germany studying the most modern laboratories and returned to plan the new building. The imposing Edward Davies Building was designed by London architect Alfred William Stephens Cross ma friba (1858-1932) who had won more than 26 national competitions and achieved a considerable reputation for designing municipal buildings. H Willcock & Co. of Wolverhampton were contracted to build the laboratories and its interior fittings. A furnished museum and reference library was presented by Sir Henry Tate. The eventual cost of £23,000 was met in total by the Davies family and the building was opened by the Chancellor of the Exchequer, H H Asquith on 1st November 1907.

The impressive 'Wrenaissance'-style building, of a dark local stone with light wrought Grinshill stone cornices, architrave, parapet and central cupola, is set into the hillside on elevated ground overlooking the centre of town. Now a Grade II listed building, it was for many years a state-of-the-art laboratory, one of the earliest purpose-built chemical laboratories in the country and the first in Wales. The Department of Chemistry closed in 1988 as a consequence of the rationalisation of degree schemes within the University of Wales. The Visual Art Department, which had outgrown its premises on Llanbadarn Road, recognised the potential of the Edward Davies Building for expanding its undergraduate and postgraduate teaching activities and for the development of the Museum collections. It seemed most appropriate that the building should now house the art department and its collections. Three of the main benefactors to the Museum had strong ties to the building - Gwendoline and Margaret Davies had paid for its construction and Dr Elvet Lewis was former student at the Chemistry Department.

The Edward Davies Building was restored and adapted for the re-titled 'School of Art' during 1993 and was officially opened by Vice-Chancellor Kenneth O Morgan in March 1994. The move not only provided increased space for the School's activities in art and art history but it also allowed for the setting up of two galleries in the building, with access for the public as well as students, and a museum area in which to display and store some of the fine and decorative art. Such on-site facilities for the display and study of art for students were followed up with three new art history courses which involve a theoretical, historical and practical study of museums and the display and interpretation of museum objects. The courses, which are the first of their kind in Wales, have the collections at the core of their teaching. The first exhibition from the collections in the new galleries was organised by Assistant Curator Neil Holland and his students. *Curious and Out of the Way* was a re-evaluation of the Powell Bequest, the first exhibition to bring together his collections since they came to the University in 1882.

The collections still serve to 'instruct and inspire' successive generations of students, providing first-hand knowledge of original works of art, and now form an invaluable research resource for both staff and students of the School of Art. If it were not for the generous gifts and bequests of George Powell, Sir John Williams, Gwendolen and Margaret Davies, Elvet Lewis and the many hundreds of individual gifts from friends and former students, the cultural life of the University and the town would be greatly impoverished. It is with a deep sense of gratitude therefore that we acknowledge the work of the previous curators of the collections who were driven by a passionate determination to form meaningful collections and, in order to engage others with those meanings, fought to keep body and soul of the collections intact. More often than not theirs was a thankless task and one which they could not have accomplished without considerable personal cost. Despite all the set backs and inevitable failures, their vision of the future was undaunted:

The now world re-nowned University collections at the Ashmolean at Oxford and the Fitzwilliam at Cambridge each started in quite a small way and with the individual gifts of one or two collectors. Little did these pioneers dream of the great treasure stores that would result from their early efforts. So perhaps in a hundred years hence when these fine examples of Craftwork are housed in a worthy building on the Hill, those who visit them will appreciate and value very greatly the generous gifts of today.

The Curators, Annual Reports, (1926)
RM